Billy Graham's

The Bible Says

World Wide Publications
Minneapolis, Minnesota

BILLY GRAHAM'S THE BIBLE SAYS

World Wide Publications is the publishing division of the Billy Graham Evangelistic Association.

Scripture quotations marked NIV are taken from the HOLY BIBLE, NEW INTERNATIONAL VERSION. Copyright © 1973, 1978, 1984 by the International Bible Society. Used by permission of Zondervan Bible Publishers.

ISBN: 0-89066-117-0

Printed in the United States of America

This booklet containing choice selections from the Bible has been compiled to assist you in your Christian life. By experience we know the power of the Word of God, for we have felt its impact upon our own lives and have seen its message go out across vast crowds, awakening within them a sense of sin and need, and bringing them to repentance and faith in Jesus Christ.

In your Christian life you will come back again and again to these gems of spiritual truth, and they will serve as a constant source of inspiration and strength. Commit them to memory; and in your moments of relaxation, ponder them in your mind. Then when they have worked the miracle in your life, pass them on to others. They will be forever grateful to you.

Billy Graham

THE BIBLE SAYS

There is no substitute for your study of the Bible itself, no matter how many Bible study helps you may have. But many who have just begun their quest for spiritual understanding may not realize that the Bible is a library of mainly historical books—telling the history of God's dealings with man. Therefore, Bible passages on a particular topic may be dispersed throughout its many pages. For instance, verses about hope fill the Bible from beginning to end, since hope has always been an important part of God's dealings with man. *The Bible Says* arranges hundreds of Bible texts according to topic. We trust that this topical arrangement will be a useful supplement to your study of God's Word.

Here are some further suggestions as you begin exploring the treasures of God's library:

First, choose a Bible with clear type, containing a concordance and a Bible dictionary.

Second, secure one or more modern translations, such as the New International Version, the New American Standard or Good News for Modern Man. When reading, compare translations to help clarify what is being said. (All the Bible passages in this present volume are given in both the King James and the New International versions.)

Third, you may want to keep notes on things important to you. This will help you remember, even though you may later discard the notes.

Fourth, you need help in understanding these great truths, and God has provided this help for you. It is God's Spirit who is our Teacher: "As his anointing teaches you about all things and as that anointing is real, not counterfeit—just as it has taught you, remain in him" (1 John 2:27, NIV). Invite Him to help you and always depend upon His help.

Fifth, be willing and ready to obey the truth as you come upon it. He that is willing "to do His will, he shall know" (John 7:17, RSV).

Sixth, until you have become familiar with the Bible, you might like to begin by reading some of the most well-known chapters, such as John 3, John 14, Romans 8, Psalm 23, Isaiah 53, Psalm 150, Psalm 37, 1 John 1, John 10, Psalm 19, 1 Corinthians 15, Hebrews 11, 1 Thessalonians 5, Luke 24, Matthew 5-7 and Psalm 1. Then try reading entire books, beginning with John, continuing with Acts, 1 John, Philippians, Romans, Luke, Mark, Hebrews and Ephesians. In the Old Testament read Psalms, Isaiah and Proverbs. Finally, read the entire Bible through.

About Your Bible

Matthew 4:4, Deut 8:3
Man shall not live by bread alone, but by every word that proceedeth out of the mouth of God.

Joshua 1:8
This book of the law shall not depart out of thy mouth; but thou shalt meditate therein day and night, that thou mayest observe to do according to all that is written therein; for then thou shalt make thy way prosperous, and then thou shalt have good success.

Job 23:12b
I have esteemed the words of his mouth more than my necessary food.

Psalm 19:7-11
The law of the Lord is perfect, converting the soul; the testimony of the Lord is sure, making wise the simple. The statutes of the Lord are right, rejoicing the heart; the commandment of the Lord is pure, enlightening the eyes. The fear of the Lord is clean, enduring forever; the judgments of the Lord are true and righteous altogether. More to be desired are they than gold, yea, than much fine gold; sweeter also than honey and the honeycomb. Moreover by them is thy servant warned; and in keeping of them there is great reward.

Psalm 119:11, 89, 165
Thy word have I hid in mine heart, that I might not sin against thee . . . For ever, O Lord, thy word is settled in heaven . . . Great peace have they which love thy law; and nothing shall offend them.

Matthew 4:4, Deut. 8:3
Man does not live on bread alone, but on every word that comes from the mouth of God.

Joshua 1:8
Do not let this Book of the Law depart from your mouth; meditate on it day and night, so that you may be careful to do everything written in it. Then you will be prosperous and successful.

Job 23:12b
I have treasured the words of his mouth more than my daily bread.

Psalm 19:7-11
The law of the Lord is perfect, reviving the soul. The statutes of the Lord are trustworthy, making wise the simple. The precepts of the Lord are right, giving joy to the heart. The commands of the Lord are radiant, giving light to the eyes. The fear of the Lord is pure, enduring forever. The ordinances of the Lord are sure and altogether righteous. They are more precious than gold, than much pure gold; they are sweeter than honey, than honey from the comb. By them is your servant warned; in keeping them there is great reward.

Psalm 119:11,89,165
I have hidden your word in my heart that I might not sin against you . . . Your word, O Lord, is eternal; it stands firm in the heavens . . . Great peace have they who love your law, and nothing can make them stumble.

Isaiah 8:20
To the law and to the testimony; if they speak not according to this word, it is because there is no light in them.

Isaiah 40:8
The grass withereth, the flower fadeth; but the word of our God shall stand for ever.

Matthew 7:24,25
Therefore whosoever heareth these sayings of mine, and doeth them, I will liken him unto a wise man, which built his house upon a rock. And the rain descended, and the floods came, and the winds blew, and beat upon that house; and it fell not; for it was founded upon a rock.

Mark 7:9,13
And he said unto them, Full well ye reject the commandment of God, that ye may keep your own tradition . . . making the word of God of none effect through your tradition, which ye have delivered . . .

Isaiah 8:20
To the law and to the testimony! If they do not speak according
to this word, they have no light of dawn.

Isaiah 40:8
The grass withers and the flowers fall, but the word of our God
stands forever.

Matthew 7:24,25
Therefore everyone who hears these words of mine and puts them
into practice is like a wise man who built his house on the rock.
The rain came down, the streams rose, and the winds blew and
beat against that house; yet it did not fall, because it had its foundation on the rock.

Mark 7:9,13
And he said to them: "You have a fine way of setting aside the
commands of God in order to observe your own tradi-
tions!. . . Thus you nullify the word of God by your tradition
that you have handed down . . . "

The Bible Is God's Message to Us

2 Timothy 3:16,17
All Scripture is given by inspiration of God, and is profitable for doctrine, for reproof, for correction, for instruction in righteousness: that the man of God may be perfect, thoroughly furnished unto all good works.

Ephesians 6:17
And take the helmet of salvation, and the sword of the Spirit, which is the word of God.

1 Peter 1:11,12
Searching what, or what manner of time the Spirit of Christ which was in them did signify, when it testified beforehand the sufferings of Christ, and the glory that should follow. Unto whom it was revealed, that not unto themselves, but unto us they did minister the things, which are now reported unto you by them that have preached the gospel unto you with the Holy Ghost sent down from heaven; which things the angels desire to look into.

2 Peter 1:21
For the prophecy came not in old time by the will of man; but holy men of God spake as they were moved by the Holy Ghost.

Hebrews 4:12
For the word of God is quick, and powerful, and sharper than any two-edged sword, piercing even to the dividing asunder of soul and spirit, and of the joints and marrow, and is a discerner of the thoughts and intents of the heart.

2 Timothy 3:16,17
All Scripture is God-breathed and is useful for teaching, rebuking, correcting and training in righteousness, so that the man of God may be thoroughly equipped for every good work.

Ephesians 6:17
Take the helmet of salvation and the sword of the Spirit, which is the word of God.

1 Peter 1:11,12
Trying to find out the time and circumstances to which the Spirit of Christ in them was pointing when he predicted the sufferings of Christ and the glories that would follow. It was revealed to them that they were not serving themselves but you, when they spoke of the things that have now been told you by those who have preached the gospel to you by the Holy Spirit sent from heaven. Even angels long to look into these things.

2 Peter 1:21
For prophecy never had its origin in the will of man, but men spoke from God as they were carried along by the Holy Spirit.

Hebrews 4:12
The word of God is living and active. Sharper than any double-edged sword, it penetrates even to dividing soul and spirit, joints and marrow; it judges the thoughts and attitudes of the heart.

We Are Saved Through the Message of the Bible

James 1:18
Of his own will begat he us with the word of truth, that we should be a kind of firstfruits of his creatures.

1 Peter 1:23
Being born again, not of corruptible seed, but of incorruptible, by the word of God, which liveth and abideth forever.

John 6:63
It is the Spirit that quickeneth; the flesh profiteth nothing. The words that I speak unto you, they are spirit, and they are life.

Romans 10:17
So then faith cometh by hearing, and hearing by the word of God.

James 1:18
He chose to give us birth through the word of truth, that we might
be a kind of firstfruits of all he created.

1 Peter 1:23
For you have been born again, not of perishable seed, but of
imperishable, through the living and enduring word of God.

John 6:63
"The Spirit gives life; the flesh counts for nothing. The words
I have spoken to you are spirit and they are life."

Romans 10:17
Consequently, faith comes from hearing the message, and the
message is heard through the word of Christ.

The Bible Tells Us of Our Sin

Romans 7:7-13

What shall we say then? Is the law sin? God forbid. Nay, I had not known sin, but by the law; for I had not known lust, except that the law had said, Thou shalt not covet. But sin, taking occasion by the commandment, wrought in me all manner of concupiscence. For without the law sin was dead. For I was alive without the law once; but when the commandment came, sin revived, and I died. And the commandment, which was ordained to life, I found to be unto death. For sin, taking occasion by the commandment, deceived me, and by it slew me. Wherefore the law is holy, and the commandment holy, and just, and good. Was then that which is good made death unto me? God forbid. But sin, that it might appear sin, working death in me by that which is good; that sin by the commandment might become exceeding sinful.

4

Romans 7:7-13

What shall we say, then? Is the law sin? Certainly not! Indeed I would not have known what sin was except through the law. For I would not have known what it was to covet if the law had not said, "Do not covet." But sin, seizing the opportunity afforded by the commandment, produced in me every kind of covetous desire. For apart from law, sin is dead. Once I was alive apart from law; but when the commandment came, sin sprang to life and I died. I found that the very commandment that was intended to bring life actually brought death. For sin, seizing the opportunity afforded by the commandment, deceived me, and through the commandment put me to death. So then, the law is holy, and the commandment is holy, righteous and good. Did that which is good, then, become death to me? By no means! But in order that sin might be recognized as sin, it produced death in me through what was good, so that through the commandment sin might become utterly sinful.

How Sin Began

Genesis 2:16,17
And the Lord God commanded the man, saying, Of every tree of
the garden thou mayest freely eat. But of the tree of the knowledge
of good and evil, thou shalt not eat of it; for in the day that thou
eatest thereof thou shalt surely die.

Genesis 3:4-6
And the serpent said unto the woman, Ye shall not surely die. For
God doth know that in the day ye eat thereof, then your eyes shall
be opened, and ye shall be as gods, knowing good and evil. And
when the woman saw that the tree was good for food, and that it
was pleasant to the eyes, and a tree to be desired to make one wise,
she took of the fruit thereof, and did eat, and gave also unto her
husband with her; and he did eat.

2 Corinthians 11:3,14,15
But I fear, lest by any means, as the serpent beguiled Eve through
his subtilty, so your minds should be corrupted from the simplicity
that is in Christ . . . And no marvel; for Satan himself is transformed
into an angel of light. Therefore it is no great thing if his ministers
also be transformed as the ministers of righteousness; whose end
shall be according to their works.

Genesis 3:16-19
Unto the woman he said, I will greatly multiply thy sorrow and thy
conception; in sorrow thou shalt bring forth children; and thy desire
shall be to thy husband, and he shall rule over thee. And unto Adam
he said, Because thou hast hearkened unto the voice of thy wife,
and hast eaten of the tree, of which I commanded thee, saying, Thou
shalt not eat of it, cursed is the ground for thy sake; in sorrow shalt

Genesis 2:16,17
And the Lord God commanded the man, "You are free to eat from any tree in the garden; but you must not eat from the tree of the knowledge of good and evil, for when you eat of it you will surely die."

Genesis 3:4-6
"You will not surely die," the serpent said to the woman. "For God knows that when you eat of it your eyes will be opened, and you will be like God, knowing good and evil." When the woman saw that the fruit of the tree was good for food and pleasing to the eye, and also desirable for gaining wisdom, she took some and ate it. She also gave some to her husband, who was with her, and he ate it.

2 Corinthians 11:3,14,15
But I am afraid that just as Eve was deceived by the serpent's cunning, your minds may somehow be led astray from your sincere and pure devotion to Christ . . . And no wonder, for Satan himself masquerades as an angel of light. It is not surprising, then, if his servants masquerade as servants of righteousness. Their end will be what their actions deserve.

Genesis 3:16-19
To the woman he said, "I will greatly increase your pains in childbearing; with pain you will give birth to children. Your desire will be for your husband, and he will rule over you." To Adam he said, "Because you listened to your wife and ate from the tree about which I commanded you, 'You must not eat of it,' Cursed is the ground because of you; through painful toil you will

thou eat of it all the days of thy life. Thorns also and thistles shall it bring forth to thee; and thou shalt eat the herb of the field. In the sweat of thy face shalt thou eat bread, till thou return unto the ground; for out of it wast thou taken; for dust thou art, and unto dust shalt thou return.

1 Corinthians 15:22, 45-49

For as in Adam all die, even so in Christ shall all be made alive . . . And so it is written, The first man Adam was made a living soul; the last Adam was made a quickening spirit. Howbeit that was not first which is spiritual, but that which is natural; and afterward that which is spiritual. The first man is of the earth, earthy; the second man is the Lord from heaven. As is the earthy, such are they also that are earthy; and as is the heavenly, such are they also that are heavenly. And as we have borne the image of the earthy, we shall also bear the image of the heavenly.

Romans 5:12, 17-19

Wherefore, as by one man sin entered into the world, and death by sin; and so death passed upon all men, for that all have sinned . . . if by one man's offense death reigned by one; much more they which receive abundance of grace and of the gift of righteousness shall reign in life by one, Jesus Christ. Therefore, as by the offense of one judgment came upon all men to condemnation; even so by the righteousness of one the free gift came upon all men unto justification of life. For as by one man's disobedience many were made sinners, so by the obedience of one shall many be made righteous.

eat of it all the days of your life. It will produce thorns and thistles
for you, and you will eat the plants of the field. By the sweat
of your brow you will eat your food until you return to the ground,
since from it you were taken; for dust you are and to dust you
will return."

1 Corinthians 15:22,45-49
For as in Adam all die, so in Christ all will be made alive . . . So
it is written: "The first man Adam became a living being"; the
last Adam, a life-giving spirit. The spiritual did not come first,
but the natural, and after that the spiritual. The first man was
of the dust of the earth, the second man from heaven. As was
the earthly man, so are those who are of the earth; and as is
the man from heaven, so also are those who are of heaven. And
just as we have borne the likeness of the earthly man, so shall
we bear the likeness of the man from heaven.

Romans 5:12,17-19
Therefore, just as sin entered the world through one man, and
death through sin, and in this way death came to all men, because
all sinned . . . For if, by the trespass of the one man, death reigned through that one man, how much more will those who receive
God's abundant provision of grace and of the gift of righteousness
reign in life through the one man, Jesus Christ. Consequently,
just as the result of one trespass was condemnation for all men,
so also the result of one act of righteousness was justification
that brings life for all men. For just as through the disobedience
of the one man the many were made sinners, so also through
the obedience of the one man the many will be made righteous.

The Effects of Sin

Isaiah 48:22
There is no peace, saith the Lord, unto the wicked.

Isaiah 57:20
But the wicked are like the troubled sea, when it cannot rest, whose
waters cast up mire and dirt.

Matthew 15:19,20
For out of the heart proceed evil thoughts, murders, adulteries, for-
nications, thefts, false witness, blasphemies . . . These are the things
which defile a man; but to eat with unwashen hands defileth not
a man.

Romans 3:10-18
As it is written, There is none righteous, no, not one. There is none
that understandeth, there is none that seeketh after God. They are
all gone out of the way, they are together become unprofitable; there
is none that doeth good, no, not one. Their throat is an open
sepulchre; with their tongues they have used deceit; the poison of
asps is under their lips; whose mouth is full of cursing and bitterness.
Their feet are swift to shed blood; destruction and misery are in
their ways; and the way of peace have they not known. There is no
fear of God before their eyes.

Galatians 5:19-21
Now the works of the flesh are manifest, which are these; Adultery,
fornication, uncleanness, lasciviousness, idolatry, witchcraft, hatred,
variance, emulations, wrath, strife, seditions, heresies, envyings,
murders, drunkenness, revelings, and such like; of the which I tell
you before, as I have also told you in time past, that they which

Isaiah 48:22
"There is no peace," says the Lord, "for the wicked."

Isaiah 57:20
But the wicked are like the tossing sea, which cannot rest, whose waves cast up mire and mud.

Matthew 15:19,20
"For out of the heart come evil thoughts, murder, adultery, sexual immorality, theft, false testimony, slander. These are what make a man 'unclean'; but eating with unwashed hands does not make him 'unclean.' "

Romans 3:10-18
As it is written: "There is no one righteous, not even one; there is no one who understands, no one who seeks God. All have turned away, they have together become worthless; there is no one who does good, not even one. Their throats are open graves; their tongues practice deceit. The poison of vipers is on their lips. Their mouths are full of cursing and bitterness. Their feet are swift to shed blood; ruin and misery mark their ways, and the way of peace they do not know. There is no fear of God before their eyes."

Galatians 5:19-21
The acts of the sinful nature are obvious: sexual immorality, impurity and debauchery; idolatry and witchcraft; hatred, discord, jealousy, fits of rage, selfish ambition, dissensions, factions and envy; drunkenness, orgies, and the like. I warn you, as I did before, that those who live like this will not inherit the kingdom

do such things shall not inherit the kingdom of God.

Romans 8:20-23
For the creature was made subject to vanity, not willingly, but by reason of him who hath subjected the same in hope, because the creature itself also shall be delivered from the bondage of corruption into the glorious liberty of the children of God. For we know that the whole creation groaneth and travaileth in pain together until now. And not only they, but ourselves also, which have the firstfruits of the Spirit, even we ourselves groan within ourselves, waiting for the adoption, to wit, the redemption of our body.

of God.

Romans 8:20-23
For the creation was subjected to frustration, not by its own choice, but by the will of the one who subjected it, in hope that the creation itself will be liberated from its bondage to decay and brought into the glorious freedom of the children of God. We know that the whole creation has been groaning as in the pains of childbirth right up to the present time. Not only so, but we ourselves, who have the firstfruits of the Spirit, groan inwardly as we wait eagerly for our adoption as sons, the redemption of our bodies.

The Helplessness of the Sinner

Proverbs 16:25
There is a way that seemeth right unto a man; but the end thereof are the ways of death.

Jeremiah 17:9
The heart is deceitful above all things, and desperately wicked; who can know it?

Jeremiah 13:23
Can the Ethiopian change his skin, or the leopard his spots? Then may ye also do good, that are accustomed to do evil.

Jeremiah 2:22
For though thou wash thee with nitre, and take thee much soap, yet thine iniquity is marked before me, saith the Lord God.

Isaiah 64:6
But we are all as an unclean thing, and all our righteousnesses are as filthy rags; and we all do fade as a leaf; and our iniquities, like the wind, have taken us away.

Romans 5:6
For when we were yet without strength, in due time Christ died for the ungodly.

Romans 8:8
So then they that are in the flesh cannot please God.

Proverbs 16:25
There is a way that seems right to a man but in the end it leads to death.

Jeremiah 17:9
The heart is deceitful above all things and beyond cure. Who can understand it?

Jeremiah 13:23
Can the Ethiopian change his skin or the leopard its spots? Neither can you do good who are accustomed to doing evil.

Jeremiah 2:22
"Although you wash yourself with soda and use an abundance of soap, the stain of your guilt is still before me," declares the Sovereign Lord.

Isaiah 64:6
All of us have become like one who is unclean, and all our righteous acts are like filthy rags; we all shrivel up like a leaf, and like the wind our sins sweep us away.

Romans 5:6
You see, at just the right time, when we were still powerless, Christ died for the ungodly.

Romans 8:8
Those controlled by the sinful nature cannot please God.

Ephesians 2:1-5
And you hath he quickened, who were dead in trespasses and sins;
wherein in time past ye walked according to the course of this world,
according to the prince of the power of the air, the spirit that now
worketh in the children of disobedience. Among whom also we all
had our conversation in times past in the lusts of our flesh, fulfilling the desires of the flesh and of the mind; and were by nature
the children of wrath, even as others. But God, who is rich in mercy, for his great love wherewith he loved us, even when we were
dead in sins, hath quickened us together with Christ, (by grace ye
are saved;) . . .

Romans 7:14-20

For we know that the law is spiritual; but I am carnal, sold under
sin. For that which I do, I allow not; for what I would, that do I
not; but what I hate, that do I. If then I do that which I would not,
I consent unto the law that it is good. Now then it is no more I that
do it, but sin that dwelleth in me. For I know that in me (that is,
in my flesh,) dwelleth no good thing; for to will is present with
me; but how to perform that which is good I find not. For the good
that I would, I do not; but the evil which I would not, that I do.
Now if I do that I would not, it is no more I that do it, but sin that
dwelleth in me.

Ephesians 2:1-5
As for you, you were dead in your transgressions and sins, in which you used to live when you followed the ways of this world and of the ruler of the kingdom of the air, the spirit who is now at work in those who are disobedient. All of us also lived among them at one time, gratifying the cravings of our sinful nature and following its desires and thoughts. Like the rest, we were by nature objects of wrath. But because of his great love for us, God, who is rich in mercy, made us alive with Christ even when we were dead in transgressions—it is by grace you have been saved.

Romans 7:14-20
We know that the law is spiritual; but I am unspiritual, sold as a slave to sin. I do not understand what I do. For what I want to do I do not do, but what I hate I do. And if I do what I do not want to do, I agree that the law is good. As it is, it is no longer I myself who do it, but it is sin living in me. I know that nothing good lives in me, that is, in my sinful nature. For I have the desire to do what is good, but I cannot carry it out. For what I do is not the good I want to do; no, the evil I do not want to do—this I keep on doing. Now if I do what I do not want to do, it is no longer I who do it, but it is sin living in me that does it.

What Jesus Did for Sinners

Matthew 1:21
And she shall bring forth a son, and thou shalt call his name JESUS; for he shall save his people from their sins.

1 Timothy 1:15
This is a faithful saying, and worthy of all acceptation, that Christ Jesus came into the world to save sinners . . .

Luke 19:10
For the Son of man is come to seek and to save that which was lost.

Galatians 4:4,5
But when the fulness of the time was come, God sent forth his Son, made of a woman, made under the law, to redeem them that were under the law, that we might receive the adoption of sons.

a. He Died for Our Sins

1 Corinthians 15:3
For I delivered unto you first of all that which I also received, how that Christ died for our sins according to the Scriptures.

Galatians 1:4
Who gave himself for our sins, that he might deliver us from this present evil world, according to the will of God and our Father.

Revelation 1:5
And from Jesus Christ, who is the faithful witness, and the first begotten of the dead, and the prince of the kings of the earth. Unto

Matthew 1:21
"She will give birth to a son, and you are to give him the name Jesus, because he will save his people from their sins."

1 Timothy 1:15
Here is a trustworthy saying that deserves full acceptance: Christ Jesus came into the world to save sinners—of whom I am the worst.

Luke 19:10
"For the Son of Man came to seek and to save what was lost."

Galatians 4:4,5
But when the time had fully come, God sent his Son, born of a woman, born under law, to redeem those under law, that we might receive the full rights of sons.

a. He Died for Our Sins

1 Corinthians 15:3
For what I received I passed on to you as of first importance: that Christ died for our sins according to the Scriptures.

Galatians 1:4
Who gave himself for our sins to rescue us from the present evil age, according to the will of our God and Father.

Revelation 1:5
And from Jesus Christ, who is the faithful witness, the firstborn from the dead, and the ruler of the kings of the earth. To him

him that loved us, and washed us from our sins in his own blood.

Hebrews 10:10,12,14
By the which will we are sanctified through the offering of the body of Jesus Christ once for all . . . but this man, after he had offered one sacrifice for sins for ever, sat down on the right hand of God . . . For by one offering he hath perfected for ever them that are sanctified.

John 19:16-18
. . . And they took Jesus . . . and he bearing his cross went forth into a place called the place of a skull, which is called in the Hebrew Golgotha; where they crucified him, and two others with him, on either side one, and Jesus in the midst.

Acts 2:22,23
Ye men of Israel, hear these words; Jesus of Nazareth, a man approved of God among you by miracles and wonders and signs, which God did by him in the midst of you, as ye yourselves also know; him, being delivered by the determinate counsel and foreknowledge of God, ye have taken, and by wicked hands have crucified and slain.

1 Corinthians 2:7,8
But we speak the wisdom of God in a mystery, even the hidden wisdom, which God ordained before the world unto our glory; which none of the princes of this world knew; for had they known it, they would not have crucified the Lord of glory.

Romans 4:25
Who was delivered for our offenses, and was raised again for our justification.

Romans 5:8
But God commendeth his love toward us, in that while we were yet sinners, Christ died for us.

John 10:11,18
I am the good shepherd; the good shepherd giveth his life for the sheep . . . No man taketh it from me, but I lay it down of myself. I have power to lay it down, and I have power to take it again . . .

who loves us and has freed us from our sins by his blood.

Hebrews 10:10,12,14
And by that will, we have been made holy through the sacrifice of the body of Jesus Christ once for all . . . But when this priest had offered for all time one sacrifice for sins, he sat down at the right hand of God . . . because by one sacrifice he has made perfect forever those who are being made holy.

John 19:16-18
So the soldiers took charge of Jesus. Carrying his own cross, he went out to The Place of the Skull (which in Aramaic is called Golgotha). Here they crucified him, and with him two others—one on each side and Jesus in the middle.

Acts 2:22,23
"Men of Israel, listen to this: Jesus of Nazareth was a man accredited by God to you by miracles, wonders and signs, which God did among you through him, as you yourselves know. This man was handed over to you by God's set purpose and foreknowledge; and you, with the help of wicked men, put him to death by nailing him to the cross."

1 Corinthians 2:7,8
No, we speak of God's secret wisdom, a wisdom that has been hidden and that God destined for our glory before time began. None of the rulers of this age understood it, for if they had, they would not have crucified the Lord of glory.

Romans 4:25
He was delivered over to death for our sins and was raised to life for our justification.

Romans 5:8
But God demonstrates his own love for us in this: While we were still sinners, Christ died for us.

John 10:11,18
"I am the good shepherd. The good shepherd lays down his life for the sheep . . . No one takes it from me, but I lay it down of my own accord. I have authority to lay it down and authority

b. He Rose for Our Justification

Romans 4:25
Who was delivered for our offenses, and was raised again for our justification.

Romans 6:9,10
Knowing that Christ being raised from the dead dieth no more; death hath no more dominion over him. For in that he died, he died unto sin once; but in that he liveth, he liveth unto God.

1 Corinthians 15:3-6
. . . Christ died for our sins according to the Scriptures . . . and that he rose again the third day according to the Scriptures; and that he was seen of Cephas, then of the twelve. After that, he was seen of above five hundred brethren at once . . .

Luke 24:1-3
Now upon the first day of the week, very early in the morning, they came unto the sepulchre, bringing the spices which they had prepared . . . and they found the stone rolled away from the sepulchre. And they entered in, and found not the body of the Lord Jesus.

Acts 2:24,32
Whom God hath raised up, having loosed the pains of death; because it was not possible that he should be holden of it . . . This Jesus hath God raised up, whereof we all are witnesses.

c. He Lives to Intercede for Us

Romans 5:9,10
Much more then, being now justified by his blood, we shall be saved from wrath through him. For if, when we were enemies, we were reconciled to God by the death of his Son; much more, being reconciled, we shall be saved by his life.

to take it up again."

b. He Rose for Our Justification

Romans 4:25
He was delivered over to death for our sins and was raised to life for our justification.

Romans 6:9,10
For we know that since Christ was raised from the dead, he cannot die again; death no longer has mastery over him. The death he died, he died to sin once for all; but the life he lives, he lives to God.

1 Corinthians 15:3-6
Christ died for our sins according to the Scriptures . . . that he was raised on the third day according to the Scriptures, and that he appeared to Peter, and then to the Twelve. After that, he appeared to more than five hundred of the brothers at the same time . . .

Luke 24:1-3
On the first day of the week, very early in the morning, the women took the spices they had prepared and went to the tomb. They found the stone rolled away from the tomb, but when they entered, they did not find the body of the Lord Jesus.

Acts 2:24,32
But God raised him from the dead, freeing him from the agony of death, because it was impossible for death to keep its hold on him . . . God has raised this Jesus to life, and we are all witnesses of the fact.

c. He Lives to Intercede for Us

Romans 5:9,10
Since we have now been justified by his blood, how much more shall we be saved from God's wrath through him! For if, when we were God's enemies, we were reconciled to him through the death of his Son, how much more, having been reconciled, shall

Isaiah 53:12
. . . And he bare the sin of many, and made intercession for the transgressors.

Romans 8:34
Who is he that condemneth? It is Christ that died, yea rather, that is risen again, who is even at the right hand of God, who also maketh intercession for us.

Hebrews 7:25
Wherefore he is able also to save them to the uttermost that come unto God by him, seeing he ever liveth to make intercession for them.

Hebrews 9:12,24
Neither by the blood of goats and calves, but by his own blood he entered in once into the holy place, having obtained eternal redemption for us . . . For Christ is not entered into the holy places made with hands, which are the figures of the true; but into heaven itself, now to appear in the presence of God for us.

Hebrews 4:14
Seeing then that we have a great high priest, that is passed into the heavens, Jesus the Son of God, let us hold fast our profession.

1 John 2:1
My little children, these things write I unto you that ye sin not. And if any man sin, we have an advocate with the Father, Jesus Christ the righteous.

d. He Is Coming to Receive Us

John 14:1-3
Let not your heart be troubled; ye believe in God, believe also in me. In my Father's house are many mansions; if it were not so, I would have told you. I go to prepare a place for you. And if I go, . . . I will come again, and receive you unto myself; that where I am, there ye may be also.

we be saved through his life!

Isaiah 53:12

. . . For he bore the sin of many, and made intercession for the transgressors.

Romans 8:34

Who is he that condemns? Christ Jesus, who died—more than that, who was raised to life—is at the right hand of God and is also interceding for us.

Hebrews 7:25

Therefore he is able to save completely those who come to God through him, because he always lives to intercede for them.

Hebrews 9:12,24

He did not enter by means of the blood of goats and calves; but he entered the Most Holy Place once for all by his own blood, having obtained eternal redemption . . . for Christ did not enter a man-made sanctuary that was only a copy of the true one; he entered heaven itself, now to appear for us in God's presence.

Hebrews 4:14

Therefore, since we have a great high priest who has gone through the heavens, Jesus the Son of God, let us hold firmly to the faith we profess.

1 John 2:1

My dear children, I write this to you so that you will not sin. But if anybody does sin, we have one who speaks to the Father in our defense—Jesus Christ, the Righteous One.

d. He Is Coming to Receive Us

John 14:1-3

"Do not let your hearts be troubled. Trust in God; trust also in me. In my Father's house are many rooms; if it were not so, I would have told you. I am going there to prepare a place for you. And if I go and prepare a place for you, I will come back and take you to be with me that you also may be where I am."

Acts 1:10,11
And while they looked steadfastly toward heaven as he went up, behold, two men stood by them in white apparel; which also said, Ye men of Galilee, why stand ye gazing up into heaven? This same Jesus shall so come in like manner as ye have seen him go into heaven.

1 Thessalonians 4:13-18
But I would not have you to be ignorant, brethren, concerning them which are asleep, that ye sorrow not, even as others which have no hope. For if we believe that Jesus died and rose again, even so them also which sleep in Jesus will God bring with him. For this we say unto you by the word of the Lord, that we which are alive and remain unto the coming of the Lord shall not prevent them which are asleep. For the Lord himself shall descend from heaven with a shout, with the voice of the archangel, and with the trump of God; and the dead in Christ shall rise first. Then we which are alive and remain shall be caught up together with them in the clouds, to meet the Lord in the air; and so shall we ever be with the Lord. Wherefore comfort one another with these words.

Acts 1:10,11
They were looking intently up into the sky as he was going, when suddenly two men dressed in white stood beside them. "Men of Galilee," they said, "why do you stand there looking into the sky? This same Jesus, who has been taken from you into heaven, will come back in the same way you have seen him go into heaven."

1 Thessalonians 4:13-18
Brothers, we do not want you to be ignorant about those who fall asleep, or to grieve like the rest of men, who have no hope. We believe that Jesus died and rose again and so we believe that God will bring with Jesus those who have fallen asleep in him. According to the Lord's own word, we tell you that we who are still alive, who are left till the coming of the Lord, will certainly not precede those who have fallen asleep. For the Lord himself will come down from heaven, with a loud command, with the voice of the archangel and with the trumpet call of God, and the dead in Christ will rise first. After that, we who are still alive and are left will be caught up together with them in the clouds to meet the Lord in the air. And so we will be with the Lord forever. Therefore encourage each other with these words.

Jesus Is Willing to Save

Matthew 11:28,29
Come unto me, all ye that labor and are heavy laden, and I will give you rest. Take my yoke upon you, and learn of me; for I am meek and lowly in heart; and ye shall find rest unto your souls.

John 6:37
. . . And him that cometh to me I will in no wise cast out.

2 Peter 3:9
The Lord is not slack concerning his promise, as some men count slackness; but is long-suffering to us-ward, not willing that any should perish, but that all should come to repentance.

John 3:16,17
For God so loved the world, that he gave his only begotten Son, that whosoever believeth in him should not perish, but have everlasting life. For God sent not his Son into the world to condemn the world; but that the world through him might be saved.

Revelation 3:20
Behold, I stand at the door, and knock; if any man hear my voice, and open the door, I will come in to him, and will sup with him, and he with me.

Revelation 22:17
And the Spirit and the bride say, Come. And let him that heareth say, Come. And let him that is athirst come. And whosoever will, let him take the water of life freely.

9

Matthew 11:28,29
"Come unto to me, all you who are weary and burdened, and
I will give you rest. Take my yoke upon you and learn from me,
for I am gentle and humble in heart, and you will find rest for
your souls."

John 6:37
" . . . And whoever comes to me I will never drive away."

2 Peter 3:9
The Lord is not slow in keeping his promise, as some understand slowness. He is patient with you, not wanting anyone to
perish, but everyone to come to repentance.

John 3:16,17
"For God so loved the world that he gave his one and only Son,
that whoever believes in him shall not perish but have eternal
life. For God did not send his Son into the world to condemn
the world, but to save the world through him."

Revelation 3:20
Here I am! I stand at the door and knock. If anyone hears my
voice and opens the door, I will go in and eat with him, and
he with me.

Revelation 22:17
The Spirit and the bride say, "Come!" And let him who hears
say, "Come!" Whoever is thirsty, let him come; and whoever
wishes, let him take the free gift of the water of life.

Jesus, the Only Savior

Acts 4:12
Neither is there salvation in any other; for there is none other name under heaven given among men, whereby we must be saved.

Acts 13:39
And by him all that believe are justified from all things, from which ye could not be justified by the law of Moses.

1 John 5:11
And this is the record, that God hath given to us eternal life, and this life is in his Son.

John 14:6
Jesus saith unto him, I am the way, the truth, and the life; no man cometh unto the Father, but by me.

1 John 5:12
He that hath the Son hath life; and he that hath not the Son of God hath not life.

John 8:21,24
Then said Jesus again unto them, I go my way, and ye shall seek me, and shall die in your sins; whither I go, ye cannot come . . . I said therefore unto you, that ye shall die in your sins; for if ye believe not that I am he, ye shall die in your sins.

John 10:9
I am the door; by me if any man enter in, he shall be saved.

10

Acts 4:12
Salvation is found in no one else, for there is no other name under heaven given to men by which we must be saved.

Acts 13:39
Through him everyone who believes is justified from everything you could not be justified from by the law of Moses.

1 John 5:11
And this is the testimony: God has given us eternal life, and this life is in his Son.

John 14:6
Jesus answered, "I am the way and the truth and the life. No one comes to the Father except through me."

1 John 5:12
He who has the Son has life; he who does not have the Son of God does not have life.

John 8:21,24
Once more Jesus said to them, "I am going away, and you will look for me, and you will die in your sin. Where I go, you cannot come . . . I told you that you would die in your sins; if you do not believe that I am the one I claim to be, you will indeed die in your sins."

John 10:9
"I am the gate; whoever enters through me will be saved . . . "

Salvation Is Immediate

Luke 19:9
And Jesus said unto him, This day is salvation come to this house . . .

2 Corinthians 6:2
For he saith, I have heard thee in a time accepted, and in the day of salvation have I succored thee. Behold, now is the accepted time; behold, now is the day of salvation.

Hebrews 3:15
While it is said, Today if ye will hear his voice, harden not your hearts, as in the provocation.

Acts 2:47
 . . . And the Lord added to the church daily such as should be saved.

11

Luke 19:9
Jesus said to him, "Today salvation has come to this house . . . "

2 Corinthians 6:2
For he says, "In the time of my favor I heard you, and in the day of salvation I helped you." I tell you, now is the time of God's favor, now is the day of salvation.

Hebrews 3:15
As has just been said: "Today, if you hear his voice, do not harden your hearts as you did in the rebellion."

Acts 2:47
And the Lord added to their number daily those who were being saved.

Steps Into Salvation

a. Acknowledge Sin

Psalm 51:3-5
For I ackowledge my transgressions; and my sin is ever before me.
Against thee, thee only, have I sinned, and done this evil in thy sight;
that thou mightest be justified when thou speakest, and be clear when
thou judgest. Behold, I was shapen in iniquity; and in sin did my
mother conceive me.

Ezra 9:15
O Lord God of Israel, thou art righteous; for we remain yet escaped,
as it is this day; behold, we are before thee in our trespasses; for
we cannot stand before thee because of this.

Job 9:20
If I justify myself, mine own mouth shall condemn me; if I say,
I am perfect, it shall also prove me perverse.

Psalm 69:5
O God, thou knowest my foolishness; and my sins are not hid from
thee.

1 John 1:8-10
If we say that we have no sin, we deceive ourselves, and the truth
is not in us. If we confess our sins, he is faithful and just to forgive
us our sins, and to cleanse us from all unrighteousness. If we say
that we have not sinned, we make him a liar, and his word is not in us.

a. Acknowledge Sin

Psalm 51:3-5
For I know my transgressions, and my sin is always before me.
Against you, you only, have I sinned and done what is evil in
your sight, so that you are proved right when you speak and
justified when you judge. Surely I have been a sinner from birth,
sinful from the time my mother conceived me.

Ezra 9:15
"O Lord, God of Israel, you are righteous! We are left this day
as a remnant. Here we are before you in our guilt, though because
of it not one of us can stand in your presence."

Job 9:20
"Even if I were innocent, my mouth would condemn me; if I
were blameless, it would pronounce me guilty."

Psalm 69:5
You know my folly, O God; my guilt is not hidden from you.

1 John 1:8-10
If we claim to be without sin, we deceive ourselves and the truth
is not in us. If we confess our sins, he is faithful and just and
will forgive us our sins and purify us from all unrighteousness.
If we claim we have not sinned, we make him out to be a liar
and his word has no place in our lives.

b. Repent

Luke 13:5
I tell you, Nay; but, except ye repent, ye shall all likewise perish.

Luke 15:7
I say unto you, that likewise joy shall be in heaven over one sinner
that repenteth . . .

Luke 24:47
And that repentance and remission of sins should be preached in
his name among all nations, beginning at Jerusalem.

Acts 2:38
Then Peter said unto them, Repent, and be baptized every one of
you in the name of Jesus Christ for the remission of sins, and ye
shall receive the gift of the Holy Ghost.

Acts 3:19
Repent ye therefore, and be converted, that your sins may be blotted out, when the times of refreshing shall come from the presence
of the Lord.

Acts 17:30
And the times of this ignorance God winked at; but now commandeth
all men every where to repent.

Acts 20:21
Testifying both to the Jews, and also to the Greeks, repentance toward
God, and faith toward our Lord Jesus Christ.

Hosea 6:1
Come, and let us return unto the Lord; for he hath torn, and he
will heal us; he hath smitten, and he will bind us up.

Luke 15:17-20
And when he came to himself, he said, How many hired servants
of my father's have bread enough and to spare, and I perish with
hunger! I will arise and go to my father, and will say unto him,
Father, I have sinned against heaven, and before thee, and am no

b. Repent

Luke 13:5
"I tell you, no! But unless you repent, you too will all perish."

Luke 15:7
"I tell you that in the same way there is more rejoicing in heaven over one sinner who repents . . . "

Luke 24:47
"And repentance and forgiveness of sins will be preached in his name to all nations, beginning at Jerusalem."

Acts 2:38
Peter replied, "Repent and be baptized, every one of you, in the name of Jesus Christ so that your sins may be forgiven. And you will receive the gift of the Holy Spirit."

Acts 3:19
"Repent, then, and turn to God, so that your sins may be wiped out, that times of refreshing may come from the Lord, and that he may send the Christ, who has been appointed for you—even Jesus."

Acts 17:30
"In the past God overlooked such ignorance, but now he commands all people everywhere to repent."

Acts 20:21
"I have declared to both Jews and Greeks that they must turn to God in repentance and have faith in our Lord Jesus."

Hosea 6:1
"Come, let us return to the Lord. He has torn us to pieces but he will heal us; he has injured us but he will bind up our wounds."

Luke 15:17-20
"When he came to his senses, he said, 'How many of my father's hired men have food to spare, and here I am starving to death! I will set out and go back to my father and say to him: Father, I have sinned against heaven and against you. I am no longer

more worthy to be called thy son; make me as one of thy hired servants. And he arose, and came to his father . . .

1 Thessalonians 1:9,10
For they themselves show of us what manner of entering in we had
unto you, and how ye turned to God from idols to serve the living
and true God; and to wait for his Son from heaven . . .

1 Peter 2:25
For ye were as sheep going astray; but are now returned unto the
Shepherd and Bishop of your souls.

c. Believe, or Trust

Hebrews 11:6
But without faith it is impossible to please him; for he that cometh
to God must believe that he is, and that he is a rewarder of them
that diligently seek him.

Acts 16:31
And they said, Believe on the Lord Jesus Christ, and thou shalt be
saved . . .

Romans 4:16
Therefore it is of faith, that it might be by grace; to the end the
promise might be sure to all the seed; not to that only which is of
the law, but to that also which is of the faith of Abraham; who is
the father of us all.

Psalm 147:11
The Lord taketh pleasure in them that fear him, in those that hope
in his mercy.

Psalm 34:8,22
O taste and see that the Lord is good; blessed is the man that trusteth
in him . . . The Lord redeemeth the soul of his servants; and none
of them that trust in him shall be desolate (held guilty).

Galatians 3:22
But the Scripture hath concluded all under sin, that the promise by
faith of Jesus Christ might be given to them that believe.

worthy to be called your son; make me like one of your hired men.' So he got up and went to his father . . . "

1 Thessalonians 1:9,10
For they themselves report what kind of reception you gave us. They tell how you turned to God from idols to serve the living and true God, and to wait for his Son from heaven . . .

1 Peter 2:25
For you were like sheep going astray, but now you have returned to the Shepherd and Overseer of your souls.

c. Believe, or Trust

Hebrews 11:6
And without faith it is impossible to please God, because anyone who comes to him must believe that he exists and that he rewards those who earnestly seek him.

Acts 16:31
They replied, "Believe in the Lord Jesus, and you will be saved . . . "

Romans 4:16
Therefore, the promise comes by faith, so that it may be by grace and may be guaranteed to all Abraham's offspring—not only to those who are of the law but also to those who are of the faith of Abraham. He is the father of us all.

Psalm 147:11
The Lord delights in those who fear him, who put their hope in his unfailing love.

Psalm 34:8,22
Taste and see that the Lord is good; blessed is the man who takes refuge in him . . . The Lord redeems his servants; no one who takes refuge in him will be condemned.

Galatians 3:22
But the Scripture declares that the whole world is a prisoner of sin, so that what was promised, being given through faith in Jesus

Psalm 37:5
Commit thy way unto the Lord; trust also in him; and he shall bring
it to pass.

John 3:16
For God so loved the world, that he gave his only begotten Son,
that whosoever believeth in him should not perish, but have
everlasting life.

John 1:12
But as many as received him, to them gave he power to become
the sons of God, even to them that believe on his name.

John 3:18,36
He that believeth on him is not condemned; but he that believeth
not is condemned already, because he hath not believed in the name
of the only begotten Son of God . . . He that believeth on the Son
hath everlasting life; and he that believeth not the Son shall not see
life; but the wrath of God abideth on him.

d. Not by Works

Ephesians 2:8,9
For by grace are ye saved through faith: and that not of yourselves;
it is the gift of God; not of works, lest any man should boast.

Exodus 14:13
And Moses said unto the people, Fear ye not, stand still, and see
the salvation of the Lord, which he will show to you today . . .

John 6:44,45
No man can come to me, except the Father which hath sent me draw
him; and I will raise him up at the last day. It is written in the prophets, And they shall be all taught of God. Every man therefore
that hath heard, and hath learned of the Father, cometh unto me.

Christ, might be given to those who believe.

Psalm 37:5
Commit your way to the Lord; trust in him and he will do this.

John 3:16
"For God so loved the world that he gave his one and only Son,
that whoever believes in him shall not perish but have eternal life."

John 1:12
Yet to all who received him, to those who believed in his name,
he gave the right to become children of God.

John 3:18,36
"Whoever believes in him is not condemned, but whoever does
not believe stands condemned already because he has not believed
in the name of God's one and only Son . . . Whoever believes
in the Son has eternal life, but whoever rejects the Son will not
see life, for God's wrath remains on him."

d. Not by Works

Ephesians 2:8,9
For it is by grace you have been saved, through faith—and this
not from yourselves, it is the gift of God—not by works, so that
no one can boast.

Exodus 14:13
Moses answered the people, "Do not be afraid. Stand firm and
you will see the deliverance the Lord will bring you today. The
Egyptians you see today you will never see again."

John 6:44,45
"No one can come to me unless the Father who sent me draws
him, and I will raise him up at the last day. It is written in the
Prophets: 'They will all be taught by God.' Everyone who listens
to the Father and learns from him comes to me."

Romans 4;4,5,16
Now to him that worketh is the reward not reckoned of grace, but
of debt. But to him that worketh not, but believeth on him that
justifieth the ungodly, his faith is counted for
righteousness . . . Therefore it is of faith, that it might be by
grace . . .

2 Timothy 1:9
Who hath saved us, and called us with a holy calling, not according
to our works, but according to his own purpose and grace, which
was given us in Christ Jesus before the world began.

Titus 3:5
Not by works of righteousness which we have done, but according
to his mercy he saved us, by the washing of regeneration, and renew-
ing of the Holy Ghost.

Psalm 103:10-12
He hath not dealt with us after our sins; nor rewarded us according
to our iniquities. For as the heaven is high above the earth, so great
is his mercy toward them that fear him. As far as the east is from
the west, so far hath he removed our transgressions from us.

e. Confess Christ

Romans 10:9-11
That if thou shalt confess with thy mouth the Lord Jesus, and shalt
believe in thine heart that God hath raised him from the dead, thou
shalt be saved. For with the heart man believeth unto righteousness;
and with the mouth confession is made unto salvation. For the Scripture saith, Whosoever believeth on him shall not be ashamed.

Matthew 10:32,33
Whosoever therefore shall confess me before men, him will I confess also before my Father which is in heaven. But whosoever shall
deny me before men, him will I also deny before my Father which
is in heaven.

Romans 4:4,5,16
Now when a man works, his wages are not credited to him as a gift, but as an obligation. However, to the man who does not work but trusts God who justifies the wicked, his faith is credited as righteousness . . . Therefore, the promise comes by faith, so that it may be by grace . . .

2 Timothy 1:9
Who has saved us and called us to a holy life—not because of anything we have done but because of his own purpose and grace. This grace was given us in Christ Jesus before the beginning of time.

Titus 3:5
He saved us, not because of righteous things we had done, but because of his mercy. He saved us through the washing of rebirth and renewal by the Holy Spirit.

Psalm 103:10-12
He does not treat us as our sins deserve or repay us according to our iniquities. For as high as the heavens are above the earth, so great is his love for those who fear him; as far as the east is from the west, so far has he removed our transgressions from us.

e. Confess Christ

Romans 10:9-11
That if you confess with your mouth, "Jesus is Lord," and believe in your heart that God raised him from the dead, you will be saved. For it is with your heart that you believe and are justified, and it is with your mouth that you confess and are saved. As the Scripture says, "Everyone who trusts in him will never be put to shame."

Matthew 10:32,33
"Whoever acknowledges me before men, I will also acknowledge him before my Father in heaven. But whoever disowns me before men, I will disown him before my Father in heaven."

1 John 4:2,3,15
Hereby know ye the Spirit of God: Every spirit that confesseth that
Jesus Christ is come in the flesh is of God. And every spirit that
confesseth not that Jesus Christ is come in the flesh is not of
God . . . Whosoever shall confess that Jesus is the Son of God, God
dwelleth in him, and he in God.

Luke 24:48
And ye are witnesses of these things.

1 Peter 3:15
But sanctify the Lord God in your hearts; and be ready always to
give an answer to every man that asketh you a reason of the hope
that is in you, with meekness and fear.

1 Chronicles 16:8,9
Give thanks unto the Lord, call upon his name, make known his
deeds among the people. Sing unto him, sing psalms unto him, talk
ye of all his wondrous works.

Malachi 3:16
Then they that feared the Lord spake often one to another. And the
Lord hearkened, and heard it, and a book of remembrance was written before him for them that feared the Lord, and that thought upon
his name.

Revelation 12:11
And they overcame him by the blood of the Lamb, and by the word
of their testimony; and they loved not their lives unto the death.

1 John 4:2,3,15
This is how you can recognize the Spirit of God: Every spirit that acknowledges that Jesus Christ has come in the flesh is from God, but every spirit that does not acknowledge Jesus is not from God . . . If anyone acknowledges that Jesus is the Son of God, God lives in him and he in God.

Luke 24:48
"You are witnesses of these things."

1 Peter 3:15
But in your hearts set apart Christ as Lord. Always be prepared to give an answer to everyone who asks you to give the reason for the hope that you have. But do this with gentleness and respect.

1 Chronicles 16:8,9
Gives thanks to the Lord, call on his name; make known among the nations what he has done. Sing to him, sing praise to him; tell of all his wonderful acts.

Malachi 3:16
Then those who feared the Lord talked with each other, and the Lord listened and heard. A scroll of remembrance was written in his presence concerning those who feared the Lord and honored his name.

Revelation 12:11
"They overcame him by the blood of the Lamb and by the word of their testimony; they did not love their lives so much as to shrink from death."

The New Life in Christ

a. Conversion

Psalm 51:13
Then will I teach transgressors thy ways; and sinners shall be converted unto thee.

James 5:19,20
Brethren, if any of you do err from the truth, and one convert him, let him know that he which converteth the sinner from the error of his way shall save a soul from death, and shall hide a multitude of sins.

Matthew 18:3
. . . Verily I say unto you, Except ye be converted, and become as little children, ye shall not enter into the kingdom of heaven.

Acts 3:19
Repent ye therefore, and be converted, that your sins may be blotted out, when the times of refreshing shall come from the presence of the Lord.

b. Regeneration (the New Birth)

John 3:5,7
Jesus answered, Verily, verily, I say unto thee, Except a man be born of water and of the Spirit he cannot enter into the kingdom of God . . . Marvel not that I said unto thee, Ye must be born again.

a. Conversion

Psalm 51:13
Then I will teach transgressors your ways, and sinners will turn
back to you.

James 5:19,20
My brothers, if one of you should wander from the truth and
someone should bring him back, remember this: Whoever turns
a sinner away from his error will save him from death and cover
over a multitude of sins.

Matthew 18:3
"I tell you the truth, unless you change and become like little
children you will never enter the kingdom of heaven."

Acts 3:19
"Repent, then, and turn to God, so that your sins may be wiped
out, that times of refreshing may come from the Lord."

b. Regeneration (the New Birth)

John 3:5,7
Jesus answered, "I tell you the truth, unless a man is born of
water and the Spirit, he cannot enter the kingdom of
God . . . You should not be surprised at my saying, 'You must
be born again.' "

1 John 5:1
Whosoever believeth that Jesus is the Christ is born of God; and every one that loveth him that begat loveth him also that is begotten of him.

2 Corinthians 5:17
Therefore if any man be in Christ, he is a new creature; old things are passed away; behold, all things are become new.

Ephesians 2:1-5
And you hath he quickened, who were dead in trespasses and sins; wherein in time past ye walked according to the course of this world, according to the prince of the power of the air, the spirit that now worketh in the children of disobedience. Among whom also we all had our conversation in times past in the lust of our flesh, fulfilling the desires of the flesh and of the mind; and were by nature the children of wrath, even as others. But God, who is rich in mercy, for his great love wherewith he loved us, even when we were dead in sins, hath quickened us together with Christ . . .

Colossians 3:1
If ye then be risen with Christ, seek those things which are above . . .

1 Peter 1:23
Being born again, not of corruptible seed, but of incorruptible, by the word of God, which liveth and abideth for ever.

Romans 6:4
Therefore we are buried with him by baptism into death; that like as Christ was raised up from the dead by the glory of the Father, even so we also should walk in newness of life.

Galatians 2:20
I am crucified with Christ; nevertheless I live; yet not I, but Christ liveth in me; and the life which I now live in the flesh I live by the faith of the Son of God, who loved me, and gave himself for me.

1 John 5:1
Everyone who believes that Jesus is the Christ is born of God,
and everyone who loves the father loves his child as well.

2 Corinthians 5:17
Therefore, if anyone is in Christ, he is a new creation; the old
has gone, the new has come!

Ephesians 2:1-5
As for you, you were dead in your transgressions and sins, in
which you used to live when you followed the ways of this world
and of the ruler of the kingdom of the air, the spirit who is now
at work in those who are disobedient. All of us also lived among
them at one time, gratifying the cravings of our sinful nature
and following its desires and thoughts. Like the rest, we were
by nature objects of wrath. But because of his great love for us,
God, who is rich in mercy, made us alive with Christ even when
we were dead in transgressions—it is by grace you have been
saved.

Colossians 3:1
Since, then, you have been raised with Christ, set your hearts
on things above, where Christ is seated at the right hand of God.

1 Peter 1:23
For you have been born again, not of perishable seed, but of
imperishable, through the living and enduring word of God.

Romans 6:4
We were therefore buried with him through baptism into death
in order that, just as Christ was raised from the dead through
the glory of the Father, we too may live a new life.

Galatians 2:20
I have been crucified with Christ and I no longer live, but Christ
lives in me. The life I live in the body, I live by faith in the Son
of God, who loved me and gave himself for me.

c. Justification

Romans 3:24-28
Being justified freely by his grace through the redemption that is
in Christ Jesus; whom God hath set forth to be a propitiation through
faith in his blood, to declare his righteousness for the remission of
sins that are past, through the forbearance of God. To declare, I
say, at this time his righteousness; that he might be just, and the
justifier of him which believeth in Jesus. Where is boasting then?
It is excluded. By what law? Of works? Nay; but by the law of faith.
Therefore we conclude that a man is justified by faith without the
deeds of the law.

Galatians 2:16
Knowing that a man is not justified by the works of the law, but
by the faith of Jesus Christ, even we have believed in Jesus Christ,
that we might be justified by the faith of Christ, and not by the works
of the law. For by the works of the law shall no flesh be justified.

Isaiah 53:11
He shall see of the travail of his soul, and shall be satisfied; by his
knowledge shall my righteous servant justify many; for he shall bear
their iniquities.

d. Sanctification

John 17:17,19
Sanctify them through thy truth; thy word is truth . . . And for their
sakes I sanctify myself, that they also might be sanctified through
the truth.

1 Corinthians 1:30
But of him are ye in Christ Jesus, who of God is made unto us
wisdom, and righteousness, and sanctification, and redemption.

Ephesians 5:25-27
Husbands, love your wives, even as Christ also loved the church,
and gave himself for it; that he might sanctify and cleanse it with

c. Justification

Romans 3:24-28
And are justified freely by his grace through the redemption that
came by Christ Jesus. God presented him as a sacrifice of atone-
ment, through faith in his blood. He did this to demonstrate his
justice, because in his forbearance he had left the sins committed beforehand unpunished—he did it to demonstrate his justice
at the present time, so as to be just and the one who justifies
the man who has faith in Jesus. Where, then, is boasting? It is
excluded. On what principle? On that of observing the law? No,
but on that of faith. For we maintain that a man is justified by
faith apart from observing the law.

Galatians 2:16
Know that a man is not justified by observing the law, but by
faith in Jesus Christ. So we, too, have put our faith in Christ
Jesus that we may be justified by faith in Christ and not by observing the law, because by observing the law no one will be
justified.

Isaiah 53:11
After the suffering of his soul, he will see the light of life and
be satisfied; by his knowledge my righteous servant will justify
many, and he will bear their iniquities.

d. Sanctification

John 17:17,19
"Sanctify them by the truth; your word is truth . . . For them
I sanctify myself, that they too may be truly sanctified."

1 Corinthians 1:30
It is because of him that you are in Christ Jesus, who has become
for us wisdom from God—that is, our righteousness, holiness
and redemption.

Ephesians 5:25-27
Husbands, love your wives, just as Christ loved the church and
gave himself up for her to make her holy, cleansing her by the

the washing of water by the word, that he might present it to himself a glorious church, not having spot, or wrinkle, or any such thing; but that it should be holy and without blemish.

1 Peter 1:15,16
But as he which hath called you is holy, so be ye holy in all manner of conversation; because it is written, Be ye holy; for I am holy.

Hebrews 10:10,14
By the which will we are sanctified through the offering of the body of Jesus Christ once for all . . . For by one offering he hath perfected for ever them that are sanctified.

e. Adoption

Ephesians 1:5
Having predestinated us unto the adoption of children by Jesus Christ to himself . . .

Ephesians 3:6,15
That the Gentiles should be fellow heirs, and of the same body, and partakers of his promise in Christ by the gospel . . . Of whom the whole family in heaven and earth is named.

Romans 8:14-17,29
For as many as are led by the Spirit of God, they are the sons of God. For ye have not received the spirit of bondage again to fear; but ye have received the Spirit of adoption, whereby we cry, Abba, Father. The Spirit itself beareth witness with our spirit, that we are the children of God; and if children, then heirs; heirs of God, and joint-heirs with Christ . . . For whom he did foreknow, he also did predestinate to be conformed to the image of his Son, that he might be the firstborn among many brethren.

Hebrews 2:10,11,13
For it became him, for whom are all things, and by whom are all things, in bringing many sons unto glory, to make the captain of

washing with water through the word, and to present her to himself as a radiant church, without stain or wrinkle or any other blemish, but holy and blameless.

1 Peter 1:15,16
But just as he who called you is holy, so be holy in all you do; for it is written: "Be holy, because I am holy."

Hebrews 10:10,14
And by that will, we have been made holy through the sacrifice of the body of Jesus Christ once for all . . . because by one sacrifice he has made perfect forever those who are being made holy.

e. Adoption

Ephesians 1:5
He predestined us to be adopted as his sons through Jesus Christ, in accordance with his pleasure and will.

Ephesians 3:6,15
This mystery is that through the gospel the Gentiles are heirs together with Israel, members together of one body, and sharers together in the promise in Christ Jesus . . . from whom his whole family in heaven and on earth derives its name.

Romans 8:14-17,29
Those who are led by the Spirit of God are sons of God. For you did not receive a spirit that makes you a slave again to fear, but you received the Spirit of sonship. And by him we cry, "Abba, Father." The Spirit himself testifies with our spirit that we are God's children. Now if we are children, then we are heirs— heirs of God and co-heirs with Christ, if indeed we share in his sufferings in order that we may also share in his glory . . . for those God foreknew he also predestined to be conformed to the likeness of his Son, that he might be the firstborn among many brothers.

Hebrews 2:10,11,13
In bringing many sons to glory, it was fitting that God, for whom and through whom everything exists, should make the author

their salvation perfect through sufferings. For both he that sanctifieth and they who are sanctified are all of one; for which cause he is not ashamed to call them brethren . . . Behold I and the children which God hath given me.

f. Assurance (You Can Be Sure)

1 John 5:13
These things have I written unto you that believe on the name of the Son of God; that ye may know that ye have eternal life, and that ye may believe on the name of the Son of God.

2 Timothy 1:12
. . . I know whom I have believed, and am persuaded that he is able to keep that which I have committed unto him against that day.

Romans 8:16
The Spirit itself beareth witness with our spirit, that we are the children of God.

Ephesians 3:12
In whom we have boldness and access with confidence by the faith of him.

Isaiah 32:17
And the work of righteousness shall be peace; and the effect of righteousness quietness and assurance for ever.

Hebrews 4:16
Let us therefore come boldly unto the throne of grace, that we may obtain mercy, and find grace to help in time of need.

Hebrews 6:19
Which hope we have as an anchor of the soul, both sure and steadfast, and which entereth into that within the veil.

of their salvation perfect through suffering. Both the one who makes men holy and those who are made holy are of the same family. So Jesus is not ashamed to call them brothers . . . "Here am I, and the children God has given me."

f. Assurance (You Can Be Sure)

1 John 5:13
I write these things to you who believe in the name of the Son of God so that you may know that you have eternal life.

2 Timothy 1:12
 . . . I know whom I have believed, and am convinced that he is able to guard what I have entrusted to him for that day.

Romans 8:16
The Spirit himself testifies with our spirit that we are God's children.

Ephesians 3:12
In him and through faith in him we may approach God with freedom and confidence.

Isaiah 32:17
The fruit of righteousness will be peace; the effect of righteousness will be quietness and confidence forever.

Hebrews 4:16
Let us then approach the throne of grace with confidence, so that we may receive mercy and find grace to help us in our time of need.

Hebrews 6:19
We have this hope as an anchor for the soul, firm and secure. It enters the inner sanctuary behind the curtain.

Living the Christian Life

a. Prayer

Jeremiah 33:3
Call unto me, and I will answer thee, and show thee great and mighty things, which thou knowest not.

Joel 2:32, Acts 2:21, Romans 10:13
And it shall come to pass, that whosoever shall call on the name of the Lord shall be delivered (saved).

Matthew 6:5-8
And when thou prayest, thou shalt not be as the hypocrites are; for they love to pray standing in the synogogues and in the corners of the streets, that they may be seen of men. Verily, I say unto you, They have their reward. But thou, when thou prayest, enter into thy closet and when thou hast shut thy door, pray to thy Father which is in secret; and thy Father which seeth in secret shall reward thee openly. But when ye pray, use not vain repetitions, as the heathen do; for they think that they shall be heard for their much speaking. Be not ye therefore like unto them; for your Father knoweth what things ye have need of, before ye ask him.

Psalm 145:18,19
The Lord is nigh unto all them that call upon him, to all that call upon him in truth. He will fulfil the desire of them that fear him; he also will hear their cry, and will save them.

Psalm 37:4,5
Delight thyself also in the Lord; and he shall give thee the desires of thine heart. Commit thy way unto the Lord; trust also in him;

a. Prayer

Jeremiah 33:3
"Call to me and I will answer you and tell you great and unsearchable things you do not know."

Joel 2:32, Acts 2:21, Romans 10:13
"Everyone who calls on the name of the Lord will be saved."

Matthew 6:5-8
"But when you pray, do not be like the hypocrites, for they love to pray standing in the synagogues and on the street corners to be seen by men. I tell you the truth, they have received their reward in full. When you pray, go into your room, close the door and pray to your Father, who is unseen. Then your Father, who sees what is done in secret, will reward you. And when you pray, do not keep on babbling like pagans, for they think they will be heard because of their many words. Do not be like them, for your Father knows what you need before you ask him."

Psalm 145:18,19
The Lord is near to all who call on him, to all who call on him in truth. He fulfills the desires of those who fear him; he hears their cry and saves them.

Psalm 37:4,5
Delight yourself in the Lord and he will give you the desires of your heart. Commit your way to the Lord; trust in him and he will do this.

and he shall bring it to pass.

Matthew 7:7-11
Ask, and it shall be given you; seek, and ye shall find; knock, and
it shall be opened unto you. For every one that asketh receiveth;
and he that seeketh findeth; and to him that knocketh it shall be
opened. Or what man is there of you, whom if his son ask bread,
will he give him a stone? Or if he ask a fish, will he give him a
serpent? If ye then, being evil, know how to give good gifts unto
your children, how much more shall your Father which is in heaven
give good things to them that ask him?

James 1:5-7
If any of you lack wisdom, let him ask of God, that giveth to all
men liberally, and upbraideth not; and it shall be given him. But
let him ask in faith, nothing wavering. For he that wavereth is like
a wave of the sea driven with the wind and tossed. For let not that
man think that he shall receive any thing of the Lord.

Psalm 66:18
If I regard iniquity in my heart, the Lord will not hear me.

Isaiah 65:24
And it shall come to pass, that before they call, I will answer; and
while they are yet speaking, I will hear.

Romans 8:26,27
Likewise the Spirit also helpeth our infirmities; for we know not
what we should pray for as we ought; but the Spirit itself maketh
intercession for us with groanings which cannot be uttered. And
he that searcheth the hearts knoweth what is the mind of the Spirit,
because he maketh intercession for the saints according to the will
of God.

b. Relation to Our Environment

1 John 2:15-17
Love not the world, neither the things that are in the world. If any
man love the world, the love of the Father is not in him. For all

Matthew 7:7-11
"Ask and it will be given to you; seek and you will find; knock and
the door will be opened to you. For everyone who asks receives;
he who seeks finds; and to him who knocks, the door will be opened. Which of you, if his son asks for bread, will give him a stone?
Or if he asks for a fish, will give him a snake? If you, then, though
you are evil, know how to give good gifts to your children, how
much more will your Father in heaven give good gifts to those who
ask him!"

James 1:5-7
If any of you lacks wisdom, he should ask God, who gives generously to all without finding fault, and it will be given to him. But when
he asks, he must believe and not doubt, because he who doubts is
like a wave of the sea, blown and tossed by the wind. That man
should not think he will receive anything from the Lord; he is a
double-minded man, unstable in all he does.

Psalm 66:18
If I had cherished sin in my heart, the Lord would not have listened.

Isaiah 65:24
"Before they call I will answer; while they are still speaking I will
hear."

Romans 8:26,27
In the same way, the Spirit helps us in our weakness. We do not
know what we ought to pray, but the Spirit himself intercedes for
us with groans that words cannot express. And he who searches
our hearts knows the mind of the Spirit, because the Spirit intercedes
for the saints in accordance with God's will.

b. Relation to Our Environment

1 John 2:15-17
Do not love the world or anything in the world. If anyone loves the
world, the love of the Father is not in him. For everything in the

that is in the world, the lust of the flesh, and the lust of the eyes, and the pride of life, is not of the Father, but is of the world. And the world passeth away, and the lust thereof; but he that doeth the will of God abideth for ever.

2 Peter 3:11,12
Seeing then that all these things shall be dissolved, what manner of persons ought ye to be in all holy conversation and godliness, looking for and hasting unto the coming of the day of God . . .

Philippians 2:14-16
Do all things without murmurings and disputings; that ye may be blameless and harmless, the sons of God, without rebuke, in the midst of a crooked and perverse nation, among whom ye shine as lights in the world; holding forth the word of life . . .

1 Peter 2:11,12
Dearly beloved, I beseech you as strangers and pilgrims, abstain from fleshly lusts, which war against the soul; having your conversation honest among the Gentiles; that, whereas they speak against you as evildoers, they may by your good works, which they shall behold, glorify God in the day of visitation.

2 Corinthians 6:14-18; 7:1
Be ye not unequally yoked together with unbelievers; for what fellowship hath righteousness with unrighteousness? And what communion hath light with darkness? And what concord hath Christ with Belial? Or what part hath he that believeth with an infidel? And what agreement hath the temple of God with idols? For ye are the temple of the living God; as God hath said, I will dwell in them, and walk in them; and I will be their God, and they shall be my people. Wherefore come out from among them, and be ye separate, saith the Lord, and touch not the unclean thing; and I will receive you, and will be a Father unto you, and ye shall be my sons and daughters, saith the Lord Almighty. Having therefore these promises, dearly beloved, let us cleanse ourselves from all filthiness of the flesh and spirit, perfecting holiness in the fear of God.

world—the cravings of sinful man, the lust of his eyes and the boasting of what he has and does—comes not from the Father but from the world. The world and its desires pass away, but the man who does the will of God lives forever.

2 Peter 3:11,12
Since everything will be destroyed in this way, what kind of people ought you to be? You ought to live holy and godly lives as you look forward to the day of God and speed its coming . . .

Philippians 2:14-16
Do everything without complaining or arguing, so that you may become blameless and pure, children of God without fault in a crooked and depraved generation, in which you shine like stars in the universe as you hold out the word of life—in order that I may boast on the day of Christ that I did not run or labor for nothing.

1 Peter 2:11,12
Dear friends, I urge you, as aliens and strangers in the world, to abstain from sinful desires, which war against your soul. Live such good lives among the pagans that, though they accuse you of doing wrong, they may see your good deeds and glorify God on the day he visits us.

2 Corinthians 6:14-18; 7:1
Do not be yoked together with unbelievers. For what do righteousness and wickedness have in common? Or what fellowship can light have with darkness? What harmony is there between Christ and Belial? What does a believer have in common with an unbeliever? What agreement is there between the temple of God and idols? For we are the temple of the living God. As God has said: "I will live with them and walk among them, and I will be their God, and they will be my people." "Therefore come out from them and be separate," says the Lord. "Touch no unclean thing, and I will receive you. I will be a Father to you, and you will be my sons and daughters," says the Lord Almighty. Since we have these promises, dear friends, let us purify ourselves from everything that contaminates body and spirit, perfecting holiness out of reverence for God.

c. The Church

1 Corinthians 3:9,11
For we are laborers together with God . . . ye are God's building.
For other foundation can no man lay than that is laid, which is Jesus
Christ.

Acts 2:41,42
Then they that gladly received his word were baptized; and the same
day there were added unto them about three thousand souls. And
they continued steadfastly in the apostles' doctrine and fellowship,
and in breaking of bread, and in prayers.

Ephesians 1:22,23
And hath put all things under his feet, and gave him to be the head
over all things to the church, which is his body, the fulness of him
that filleth all in all.

1 Corinthians 12:12,13
For as the body is one, and hath many members, and all the members
of that one body, being many, are one body; so also is Christ. For
by one Spirit are we all baptized into one body, whether we be Jews
or Gentiles, whether we be bond or free; and have been all made
to drink into one Spirit.

1 Peter 2:5
Ye also, as lively stones, are built up a spiritual house, an holy
priesthood, to offer up spiritual sacrifices . . .

Hebrews 10:25
Not forsaking the assembling of ourselves together, as the manner
of some is; but exhorting one another; and so much the more, as
ye see the day approaching.

c. The Church

1 Corinthians 3:9,11
For we are God's fellow workers; you are God's field, God's building . . . For no one can lay any foundation other than the one already laid, which is Jesus Christ.

Acts 2:41,42
Those who accepted his message were baptized, and about three thousand were added to their number that day. They devoted themselves to the apostles' teaching and to the fellowship, to the breaking of bread and to prayer.

Ephesians 1:22,23
And God placed all things under his feet and appointed him to be head over everything for the church, which is his body, the fullness of him who fills everything in every way.

1 Corinthians 12:12,13
The body is a unit, though it is made up of many parts; and though all its parts are many, they form one body. So it is with Christ. For we were all baptized by one Spirit into one body—whether Jews or Greeks, slave or free—and we were all given the one Spirit to drink.

1 Peter 2:5
You also, like living stones, are being built into a spiritual house to be a holy priesthood, offering spiritual sacrifices . . .

Hebrews 10:25
Let us not give up meeting together, as some are in the habit of doing, but let us encourage one another—and all the more as you see the Day approaching.

d. *Baptism*

Matthew 28:19
Go ye therefore, and teach all nations, baptizing them in the name of the Father, and of the Son, and of the Holy Ghost.

Acts 8:12
But when they believed Philip preaching the things concerning the kingdom of God, and the name of Jesus Christ, they were baptized, both men and women.

Acts 8:36-38
And as they went on their way, they came unto a certain water. And the eunuch said, See, here is water; what doth hinder me to be baptized? And Philip said, If thou believest with all thine heart, thou mayest. And he answered and said, I believe that Jesus Christ is the Son of God. And he commanded the chariot to stand still; and they went down both into the water, both Philip and the eunuch; and he baptized him.

Romans 6:3,4
Know ye not, that so many of us as were baptized into Jesus Christ were baptized into his death? Therefore we are buried with him by baptism into death; that like as Christ was raised up from the dead by the glory of the Father, even so we also should walk in newness of life.

Ephesians 4:5
One Lord, one faith, one baptism.

e. *The Lord's Supper*

Luke 22:17-20
And he took the cup, and gave thanks, and said, Take this, and divide it among yourselves; for I say unto you, I will not drink of the fruit of the vine, until the kingdom of God shall come. And he took bread, and gave thanks, and brake it, and gave unto them, saying, This is my body which is given for you; this do in remembrance of me. Likewise also the cup after supper, saying, This cup is the new testament in my blood, which is shed for you.

d. Baptism

Matthew 28:19
"Therefore go and make disciples of all nations, baptizing them in the name of the Father and of the Son and of the Holy Spirit."

Acts 8:12
But when they believed Philip as he preached the good news of the kingdom of God and the name of Jesus Christ, they were baptized, both men and women.

Acts 8:36,38
As they traveled along the road, they came to some water and the eunuch said, "Look, here is water. Why shouldn't I be baptized?" And he ordered the chariot to stop. Then both Philip and the eunuch went down into the water and Philip baptized him.

Romans 6:3,4
Or don't you know that all of us who were baptized into Christ Jesus were baptized into his death? We were therefore buried with him through baptism into death in order that, just as Christ was raised from the dead through the glory of the Father, we too may live a new life.

Ephesians 4:5
One Lord, one faith, one baptism.

e. The Lord's Supper

Luke 22:17-20
After taking the cup, he gave thanks and said, "Take this and divide it among you. For I tell you I will not drink again of the fruit of the vine until the kingdom of God comes." And he took bread, gave thanks and broke it, and gave it to them, saying, "This is my body given for you; do this in remembrance of me." In the same way, after the supper he took the cup, saying, "This cup is the new covenant in my blood, which is poured out for you."

Acts 2:42
And they continued steadfastly in the apostles' doctrine and
fellowship, and in breaking of bread, and in prayers.

1 Corinthians 10:16,17
The cup of blessing which we bless, is it not the communion of
the blood of Christ? The bread which we break, is it not the communion of the body of Christ? For we being many are one bread,
and one body; for we are all partakers of that one bread.

1 Corinthians 11:23-26
For I have received of the Lord that which also I delivered unto
you, That the Lord Jesus the same night in which he was betrayed,
took bread; and when he had given thanks, he brake it, and said,
Take, eat; this is my body, which is broken for you; this do in remembrance of me. After the same manner also he took the cup, when
he had supped, saying, This cup is the new testament in my blood;
this do ye, as oft as ye drink it, in remembrance of me. For as often
as ye eat this bread, and drink this cup, ye do show the Lord's death
till he come.

f. Stewardship

Deuteronomy 8:11-17
Beware that thou forget not the Lord thy God, . . . lest when thou
hast eaten and art full, and hast built goodly houses, . . . then thine
heart be lifted up, and thou forget the Lord thy God . . . who led
thee . . . who fed thee . . . and thou say in thine heart, My power
and the might of mine hand hath gotten me this wealth. But thou
shalt remember the Lord thy God; for it is he that giveth thee power
to get wealth . . .

2 Corinthians 8:5,9,12,15
 . . . but first gave their own selves to the Lord . . . For ye know
the grace of our Lord Jesus Christ, that, though he was rich, yet
for your sakes he became poor, that ye through his poverty might
be rich . . . For if there be first a willing mind, it is accepted according to that a man hath, and not according to that he hath
not . . . He that had gathered much had nothing over; and he that

Acts 2:42
They devoted themselves to the apostles' teaching and to the
fellowship, to the breaking of bread and to prayer.

1 Corinthians 10:16,17
Is not the cup of thanksgiving for which we give thanks a participation in the blood of Christ? And is not the bread that we break a
participation in the body of Christ? Because there is one loaf, we,
who are many, are one body, for we all partake of the one loaf.

1 Corinthians 11:23-26
For I received from the Lord what I also passed on to you: The
Lord Jesus, on the night he was betrayed, took bread, and when
he had given thanks, he broke it and said, "This is my body, which
is for you; do this in remembrance of me." In the same way, after
supper he took the cup, saying, "This cup is the new covenant in
my blood; do this, whenever you drink it, in remembrance of me."
For whenever you eat this bread and drink this cup, you proclaim
the Lord's death until he comes.

f. Stewardship

Deuteronomy 8:11-17
Be careful that you do not forget the Lord your God, . . . Other-
wise, when you eat and are satisfied, when you build fine
houses, . . . then your heart will become proud and you will forget
the Lord your God . . . He led you . . . He gave you manna to
eat . . . You may say to yourself, "My power and the strength of
my hands have produced this wealth for me." But remember the
Lord your God, for it is he who gives you the ability to produce
wealth.

2 Corinthians 8:5,9,12.15
. . . but they gave themselves first to the Lord . . . For you know
the grace of our Lord Jesus Christ, that though he was rich, yet
for your sakes he became poor, so that you through his poverty might
become rich . . . For if the willingness is there, the gift is accep-
table according to what one has, not according to what he does not
have . . . "He that gathered much did not have too much, and he

had gathered little had no lack.

2 Corinthians 9:6,7
But this I say, He which soweth sparingly shall reap also sparingly; and he which soweth bountifully shall reap also bountifully. Every man according as he purposeth in his heart, so let him give; not grudgingly, or of necessity; for God loveth a cheerful giver.

Philippians 4:17
Not because I desire a gift; but I desire fruit that may abound to your account.

Galatians 6:6,7
Let him that is taught in the word communicate unto him that teacheth in all good things. Be not deceived; God is not mocked; for whatsoever a man soweth, that shall he also reap.

Matthew 23:23
Woe unto you, scribes and Pharisees, hypocrites! For ye pay tithe of mint and anise and cummin, and have omitted the weightier matters of the law, judgment, mercy, and faith; these ought ye to have done, and not to leave the other undone.

g. Activities and Amusements

Philippians 4:8
Finally, brethren, whatsoever things are true, whatsoever things are honest, whatsoever things are just, whatsoever things are pure, whatsoever things are lovely, whatsoever things are of good report; if there be any virtue, and if there be any praise, think on these things.

Colossians 3:1,2,17
If ye then be risen with Christ, seek those things which are above, where Christ sitteth on the right hand of God. Set your affection on things above, not on things on the earth . . . And whatsoever ye do in word or deed, do all in the name of the Lord Jesus, giving thanks to God and the Father by him.

1 Corinthians 6:19,20
What? Know ye not that your body is the temple of the Holy Ghost

that gathered little did not have too little."

2 Corinthians 9:6,7
Remember this: Whoever sows sparingly will also reap sparingly, and whoever sows generously will also reap generously. Each man should give what he has decided in his heart to give, not reluctantly or under compulsion, for God loves a cheerful giver.

Philippians 4:17
Not that I am looking for a gift, but I am looking for what may be credited to your account.

Galatians 6:6,7
Anyone who receives instruction in the word must share all good things with his instructor. Do not be deceived: God cannot be mocked. A man reaps what he sows.

Matthew 23:23
"Woe to you, teachers of the law and Pharisees, you hypocrites! You give a tenth of your spices—mint, dill and cummin. But you have neglected the more important matters of the law—justice, mercy and faithfulness. You should have practiced the latter, without neglecting the former."

g. *Activities and Amusements*

Philippians 4:8
Finally, brothers, whatever is true, whatever is noble, whatever is right, whatever is pure, whatever is lovely, whatever is admirable—if anything is excellent or praiseworthy—think about such things.

Colossians 3:1,2,17
Since, then, you have been raised with Christ, set your hearts on things above, where Christ is seated at the right hand of God. Set your minds on things above, not on earthly things . . . And whatever you do, whether in word or deed, do it all in the name of the Lord Jesus, giving thanks to God the Father through him.

1 Corinthians 6:19,20
Do you not know that your body is a temple of the Holy Spirit,

which is in you, which ye have of God, and ye are not your own? For ye are bought with a price; therefore glorify God in your body . . .

Romans 13:11-14
And that, knowing the time, that now it is high time to awake out of sleep; for now is our salvation nearer than when we believed. The night is far spent, the day is at hand; let us therefore cast off the works of darkness, and let us put on the armor of light. Let us walk honestly, as in the day; not in rioting and drunkenness, not in chambering and wantonness, not in strife and envying. But put ye on the Lord Jesus Christ, and make not provision for the flesh, to fulfil the lusts thereof.

Romans 14:19,23
Let us therefore follow after the things which make for peace, and things wherewith one may edify another . . . And he that doubteth is damned if he eat, because he eateth not of faith; for whatsoever is not of faith is sin.

h. Temptation

1 Corinthians 10:13
There hath no temptation taken you but such as is common to man; but God is faithful, who will not suffer you to be tempted above that ye are able; but will with the temptation also make a way to escape, that ye may be able to bear it.

Hebrews 4:15
For we have not an high priest which cannot be touched with the feeling of our infirmities; but was in all points tempted like as we are, yet without sin.

James 1:2-4,12-15
My brethren, count it all joy when ye fall into divers temptations; knowing this, that the trying of your faith worketh patience. But let patience have her perfect work, that ye may be perfect and entire, wanting nothing . . . Blessed is the man that endureth temptation; for when he is tried, he shall receive the crown of life, which the Lord hath promised to them that love him. Let no man say when

who is in you, whom you have received from God? You are not your own; you were bought at a price. Therefore honor God with your body.

Romans 13:11-14
And do this, understanding the present time. The hour has come for you to wake up from your slumber, because our salvation is nearer now than when we first believed. The night is nearly over; the day is almost here. So let us put aside the deeds of darkness and put on the armor of light. Let us behave decently, as in the daytime, not in orgies and drunkenness, not in sexual immorality and debauchery, not in dissension and jealousy. Rather, clothe yourselves with the Lord Jesus Christ, and do not think about how to gratify the desires of the sinful nature.

Romans 14:19,23
Let us therefore make every effort to do what leads to peace and to mutual edification . . . But the man who has doubts is condemned if he eats, because his eating is not from faith; and everything that does not come from faith is sin.

h. Temptation

1 Corinthians 10:13
No temptation has seized you except what is common to man. And God is faithful; he will not let you be tempted beyond what you can bear. But when you are tempted, he will also provide a way out so that you can stand up under it.

Hebrews 4:15
For we do not have a high priest who is unable to sympathize with our weaknesses, but we have one who has been tempted in every way, just as we are—yet was without sin.

James 1:2-4, 12-15
Consider it pure joy, my brothers, whenever you face trials of many kinds, because you know that the testing of your faith develops perseverance. Perseverance must finish its work so that you may be mature and complete, not lacking anything . . . Blessed is the man who perseveres under trial, because when he has stood the test, he will receive the crown of life that God has promised to those

he is tempted, I am tempted of God; for God cannot be tempted with evil, neither tempteth he any man. But every man is tempted, when he is drawn away of his own lust, and enticed. Then when lust hath conceived, it bringeth forth sin; and sin, when it is finished, bringeth forth death.

1 Peter 4:12
Beloved, think it not strange concerning the fiery trial which is to try you, as though some strange thing happened unto you.

Ephesians 6:11-17
Put on the whole armor of God, that ye may be able to stand against the wiles of the devil. For we wrestle not against flesh and blood, but against principalities, against powers, against the rulers of the darkness of this world, against spiritual wickedness in high places. Wherefore take unto you the whole armor of God, that ye may be able to withstand in the evil day, and having done all, to stand. Stand therefore, having your loins girt about with truth, and having on the breastplate of righteousness; and your feet shod with the preparation of the gospel of peace; above all, taking the shield of faith, wherewith ye shall be able to quench all the fiery darts of the wicked. And take the helmet of salvation, and the sword of the Spirit, which is the word of God.

i. Service

John 15:16
Ye have not chosen me, but I have chosen you, and ordained you, that ye should go and bring forth fruit, and that your fruit should remain . . .

Ephesians 2:10
For we are his workmanship, created in Christ Jesus unto good works, which God hath before ordained that we should walk in them.

Acts 1:8
But ye shall receive power, after that the Holy Ghost is come upon you; and ye shall be witnesses unto me both in Jerusalem, and in all Judea, and in Samaria, and unto the uttermost part of the earth.

who love him. When tempted, no one should say, "God is tempting me." For God cannot be tempted by evil, nor does he tempt anyone; but each one is tempted when, by his own evil desire, he is dragged away and enticed. Then, after desire has conceived, it gives birth to sin; and sin, when it is full-grown, gives birth to death.

1 Peter 4:12
Dear friends, do not be surprised at the painful trial you are suffering, as though something strange were happening to you.

Ephesians 6:11-17
Put on the full armor of God so that you can take your stand against the devil's schemes. For our struggle is not against flesh and blood, but against the rulers, against the authorities, against the powers of this dark world and against the spiritual forces of evil in the heavenly realms. Therefore put on the full armor of God, so that when the day of evil comes, you may be able to stand your ground, and after you have done everything, to stand. Stand firm then, with the belt of truth buckled around your waist, with the breastplate of righteousness in place, and with your feet fitted with the readiness that comes from the gospel of peace. In addition to all this, take up the shield of faith, with which you can extinguish all the flaming arrows of the evil one. Take the helmet of salvation and the sword of the Spirit, which is the word of God.

i. Service

John 15:16
"You did not choose me, but I chose you to go and bear fruit—fruit that will last . . . "

Ephesians 2:10
For we are God's workmanship, created in Christ Jesus to do good works, which God prepared in advance for us to do.

Acts 1:8
"But you will receive power when the Holy Spirit comes on you; and you will be my witnesses in Jerusalem, and in all Judea and Samaria, and to the ends of the earth."

Luke 24:46-49

. . . Thus it is written, and thus it behooved Christ to suffer, and to rise from the dead the third day; and that repentance and remission of sins should be preached in his name among all nations, beginning at Jerusalem. And ye are witnesses of these things. And, behold, I send the promise of my Father upon you; but tarry ye in the city of Jerusalem, until ye be endued with power from on high.

Psalm 126:6

He that goeth forth and weepeth, bearing precious seed, shall doubtless come again with rejoicing, bringing his sheaves with him.

j. Rewards for Service

Matthew 25:34

Then shall the King say unto them on his right hand, Come, ye blessed of my Father, inherit the kingdom prepared for you from the foundation of the world.

2 Timothy 4:8

Henceforth there is laid up for me a crown of righteousness, which the Lord, the righteous judge, shall give me at that day; and not to me only, but unto all them also that love his appearing.

Matthew 16:27

For the Son of man shall come in the glory of his Father with his angels; and then he shall reward every man according to his works.

Luke 6:35

But love ye your enemies, and do good, and lend, hoping for nothing again; and your reward shall be great, and ye shall be the children of the Highest; for he is kind unto the unthankful and to the evil.

Revelation 22:12

And, behold, I come quickly; and my reward is with me, to give every man according as his work shall be.

Luke 24:46-49
He told them, "This is what is written: The Christ will suffer and
rise from the dead on the third day, and repentance and forgiveness
of sins will be preached in his name to all nations, beginning at
Jerusalem. You are witnesses of these things. I am going to send
you what my Father has promised; but stay in the city until you have
been clothed with power from on high."

Psalm 126:6
He who goes out weeping, carrying seed to sow, will return with
songs of joy, carrying sheaves with him.

j. Rewards for Service

Matthew 25:34
"Then the King will say to those on his right, 'Come, you who are
blessed by my Father; take your inheritance, the kingdom prepared
for you since the creation of the world.' "

2 Timothy 4:8
Now there is in store for me the crown of righteousness, which the
Lord, the righteous Judge, will award to me on that day—and not
only to me, but also to all who have longed for his appearing.

Matthew 16:27
"For the Son of Man is going to come in his Father's glory with
his angels, and then he will reward each person according to what
he has done."

Luke 6:35
"But love your enemies, do good to them, and lend to them without
expecting to get anything back. Then your reward will be great, and
you will be sons of the Most High, because he is kind to the
ungrateful and wicked."

Revelation 22:12
"Behold, I am coming soon! My reward is with me, and I will give
to everyone according to what he has done."

The Believer's Hope for the Future

John 14:1-3
Let not your heart be troubled; ye believe in God, believe also in me. In my Father's house are many mansions; if it were not so, I would have told you. I go to prepare a place for you. And if I go and prepare a place for you, I will come again, and receive you unto myself; that where I am, there ye may be also.

Job 19:25-27
For I know that my Redeemer liveth, and that he shall stand at the latter day upon the earth. And though after my skin worms destroy this body, yet in my flesh shall I see God: whom I shall see for myself, and mine eyes shall behold, and not another; though my reins be consumed within me.

1 Thessalonians 4:13-17
But I would not have you to be ignorant, brethren, concerning them which are asleep, that ye sorrow not, even as others which have no hope. For if we believe that Jesus died and rose again, even so them also which sleep in Jesus will God bring with him. For this we say unto you by the word of the Lord, that we which are alive and remain unto the coming of the Lord shall not prevent them which are asleep. For the Lord himself shall descend from heaven with a shout, with the voice of the archangel, and with the trump of God; and the dead in Christ shall rise first. Then we which are alive and remain shall be caught up together with them in the clouds, to meet the Lord in the air; and so shall we ever be with the Lord.

1 Corinthians 15:20-22,51,52
But now is Christ risen from the dead, and become the firstfruits

15

John 14:1-3
"Do not let your hearts be troubled. Trust in God; trust also in me. In my Father's house are many rooms; if it were not so, I would have told you. I am going there to prepare a place for you. And if I go and prepare a place for you, I will come back and take you to be with me that you also may be where I am."

Job 19:25-27
"I know that my Redeemer lives, and that in the end he will stand upon the earth. And after my skin has been destroyed, yet in my flesh I will see God; I myself will see him with my own eyes—I, and not another. How my heart yearns within me!"

1 Thessalonians 4:13-17
Brothers, we do not want you to be ignorant about those who fall asleep, or to grieve like the rest of men, who have no hope. We believe that Jesus died and rose again and so we believe that God will bring with Jesus those who have fallen asleep in him. According to the Lord's own word, we tell you that we who are still alive, who are left till the coming of the Lord, will certainly not precede those who have fallen asleep. For the Lord himself will come down from heaven, with a loud command, with the voice of the archangel and with the trumpet call of God, and the dead in Christ will rise first. After that, we who are still alive and are left will be caught up with them in the clouds to meet the Lord in the air. And so we will be with the Lord forever.

1 Corinthians 15:20-22,51,52
But Christ has indeed been raised from the dead, the firstfruits of

of them that slept. For since by man came death, by man came also
the resurrection of the dead. For as in Adam all die, even so in Christ
shall all be made alive . . . Behold, I show you a mystery; We shall
not all sleep, but we shall all be changed, in a moment, in the twinkling of an eye, at the last trump. For the trumpet shall sound, and
the dead shall be raised incorruptible, and we shall be changed.

2 Corinthians 4:16-18

For which cause we faint not; but though our outward man perish,
yet the inward man is renewed day by day. For our light affliction,
which is but for a moment, worketh for us a far more exceeding
and eternal weight of glory; while we look not at the things which
are seen, but at the things which are not seen. For the things which
are seen are temporal; but the things which are not seen are eternal.

2 Corinthians 5:1-8

For we know that if our earthly house of this tabernacle were dissolved, we have a building of God, a house not made with hands, eternal in the heavens. For in this we groan, earnestly desiring to be
clothed upon with our house which is from heaven; if so be that
being clothed we shall not be found naked. For we that are in this
tabernacle do groan, being burdened; not for that we would be
unclothed, but clothed upon, that mortality might be swallowed up
of life. Now he that hath wrought us for the selfsame thing is God,
who also hath given unto us the earnest of the Spirit. Therefore we
are always confident, knowing that, whilst we are at home in the
body, we are absent from the Lord (for we walk by faith, not by
sight). We are confident, I say, and willing rather to be absent from
the body, and to be present with the Lord.

those who have fallen asleep. For since death came through a man, the resurrection of the dead comes also through a man. For as in Adam all die, so in Christ all will be made alive . . . Listen, I tell you a mystery: We will not all sleep, but we will all be changed—in a flash, in the twinkling of an eye, at the last trumpet. For the trumpet will sound, the dead will be raised imperishable, and we will be changed.

2 Corinthians 4:16-18

Therefore we do not lose heart. Though outwardly we are wasting away, yet inwardly we are being renewed day by day. For our light and momentary troubles are achieving for us an eternal glory that far outweighs them all. So we fix our eyes not on what is seen, but on what is unseen. For what is seen is temporary, but what is unseen is eternal.

2 Corinthians 5:1-8

Now we know that if the earthly tent we live in is destroyed, we have a building from God, an eternal house in heaven, not built by human hands. Meanwhile we groan, longing to be clothed with our heavenly dwelling, because when we are clothed, we will not be found naked. For while we are in this tent, we groan and are burdened, because we do not wish to be unclothed but to be clothed with our heavenly dwelling, so that what is mortal may be swallowed up by life. Now it is God who has made us for this very purpose and has given us the Spirit as a deposit, guaranteeing what is to come. Therefore we are always confident and know that as long as we are at home in the body we are away from the Lord. We live by faith, not by sight. We are confident, I say, and would prefer to be away from the body and at home with the Lord.

The Future for Those Who Know Not God

Romans 6:23
For the wages of sin is death; but the gift of God is eternal life through Jesus Christ our Lord.

Ezekiel 18:4
. . . The soul that sinneth, it shall die.

John 3:18,19
He that believeth on him is not condemned; but he that believeth not is condemned already, because he hath not believed in the name of the only begotten Son of God. And this is the condemnation, that light is come into the world, and men loved darkness rather than light, because their deeds were evil.

John 3:36
. . . He that believeth not the Son shall not see life; but the wrath of God abideth on him.

Numbers 32:23
But if ye will not do so, behold, ye have sinned against the Lord; and be sure your sin will find you out.

Luke 12:5
But I will forewarn you whom ye shall fear. Fear him, which after he hath killed hath power to cast into hell; yea, I say unto you, Fear him.

Psalm 1:4-6
The ungodly are not so; but are like the chaff which the wind driveth away. Therefore the ungodly shall not stand in the judgment, nor

16

Romans 6:23
For the wages of sin is death, but the gift of God is eternal life in Christ Jesus our Lord.

Ezekiel 18:4
" . . . The soul who sins is the one who will die."

John 3:18,19
"Whoever believes in him is not condemned, but whoever does not believe stands condemned already because he has not believed in the name of God's one and only Son. This is the verdict: Light has come into the world, but men loved darkness instead of light because their deeds were evil."

John 3:36
" . . . whoever rejects the Son will not see life, for God's wrath remains on him."

Numbers 32:23
"But if you fail to do this, you will be sinning against the Lord; and you may be sure that your sin will find you out."

Luke 12:5
"But I will show you whom you should fear: Fear him who, after the killing of the body, has power to throw you into hell. Yes, I tell you, fear him."

Psalm 1:4-6
Not so the wicked! They are like chaff that the wind blows away. Therefore the wicked will not stand in the judgment, nor sinners

sinners in the congregation of the righteous. For the Lord knoweth the way of the righteous: but the way of the ungodly shall perish.

Daniel 12:2
And many of them that sleep in the dust of the earth shall awake, some to everlasting life, and some to shame and everlasting contempt.

Matthew 13:49,50
So shall it be at the end of the world; the angels shall come forth, and sever the wicked from among the just, and shall cast them into the furnace of fire. There shall be wailing and gnashing of teeth.

Matthew 25:41,46
Then shall he say also unto them on the left hand, Depart from me, ye cursed, into everlasting fire, prepared for the devil and his angels: . . . and these shall go away into everlasting punishment; but the righteous into life eternal.

2 Thessalonians 1:7-9
And to you who are troubled rest with us, when the Lord Jesus shall be revealed from heaven with his mighty angels, in flaming fire taking vengeance on them that know not God, and that obey not the gospel of our Lord Jesus Christ; who shall be punished with everlasting destruction from the presence of the Lord, and from the glory of his power.

Revelation 21:8
But the fearful, and unbelieving, and the abominable, and murderers, and whoremongers, and sorcerers, and idolaters, and all liars, shall have their part in the lake which burneth with fire and brimstone; which is the second death.

2 Peter 3:5-7
For this they willingly are ignorant of, that by the word of God the heavens were of old, and the earth standing out of the water and in the water; whereby the world that then was, being overflowed with water, perished. But the heavens and the earth, which are now, by the same word are kept in store, reserved unto fire against the day of judgment and perdition of ungodly men.

in the assembly of the righteous. For the Lord watches over the way of the righteous, but the way of the wicked will perish.

Daniel 12:2
Multitudes who sleep in the dust of the earth will awake: some to everlasting life, others to shame and everlasting contempt.

Matthew 13:49,50
"This is how it will be at the end of the age. The angels will come and separate the wicked from the righteous and throw them into the fiery furnace, where there will be weeping and gnashing of teeth."

Matthew 25:41,46
"Then he will say to those on his left, 'Depart from me, you who are cursed, into the eternal fire prepared for the devil and his angels.' . . . Then they will go away to eternal punishment, but the righteous to eternal life."

2 Thessalonians 1:7-9
And give relief to you who are troubled, and to us as well. This will happen when the Lord Jesus is revealed from heaven in blazing fire with his powerful angels. He will punish those who do not know God and do not obey the gospel of our Lord Jesus. They will be punished with everlasting destruction and shut out from the presence of the Lord and from the majesty of his power.

Revelation 21:8
"But the cowardly, the unbelieving, the vile, the murderers, the sexually immoral, those who practice magic arts, the idolaters and all liars—their place will be in the fiery lake of burning sulfur. This is the second death."

2 Peter 3:5-7
But they deliberately forget that long ago by God's word the heavens existed and the earth was formed out of water and with water. By water also the world of that time was deluged and destroyed. By the same word the present heavens and earth are reserved for fire, being kept for the day of judgment and destruction of ungodly men.

Jude 7
Even as Sodom and Gomorrah, and the cities about them in like manner, giving themselves over to fornication, and going after strange flesh, are set forth for an example, suffering the vengeance of eternal fire.

Jude 13
Raging waves of the sea, foaming out their own shame; wandering stars, to whom is reserved the blackness of darkness for ever.

Romans 2:5-9,11-13
But, after thy hardness and impenitent heart, treasurest up unto thyself wrath against the day of wrath and revelation of the righteous judgment of God; who will render to every man according to his deeds; to them who by patient continuance in well doing seek for glory and honor and immortality, eternal life; but unto them that are contentious, and do not obey the truth, but obey unrighteousness, indignation and wrath, tribulation and anguish, upon every soul of man that doeth evil; of the Jew first, and also of the Gentile . . . For there is no respect of persons with God. For as many as have sinned without law shall also perish without law; and as many as have sinned in the law shall be judged by the law. (For not the hearers of the law are just before God, but the doers of the law shall be justified.)

Jude 7

In a similar way, Sodom and Gomorrah and the surrounding towns gave themselves up to sexual immorality and perversion. They serve as an example of those who suffer the punishment of eternal fire.

Jude 13

They are wild waves of the sea, foaming up their shame; wandering stars, for whom blackest darkness has been reserved forever.

Romans 2:5-9,11-13

But because of your stubbornness and your unrepentant heart, you are storing up wrath against yourself for the day of God's wrath, when his righteous judgment will be revealed. God "will give to each person according to what he has done." To those who by persistence in doing good seek glory, honor and immortality, he will give eternal life. But for those who are self-seeking and who reject the truth and follow evil, there will be wrath and anger. There will be trouble and distress for every human being who does evil: first for the Jew, then for the Gentile . . . For God does not show favoritism. All who sin apart from the law will also perish apart from the law, and all who sin under the law will be judged by the law. For it is not those who hear the law who are righteous in God's sight, but it is those who obey the law who will be declared righteous.

The Spirit of God and His Ministry

a. Convicts of Sin

John 16:8
And when he is come, he will reprove the world of sin, and of righteousness, and of judgment.

Acts 7:51
Ye stiffnecked and uncircumcised in heart and ears, ye do always resist the Holy Ghost . . .

Hebrews 3:7,8
Wherefore, as the Holy Ghost saith, Today if ye will hear his voice, harden not your hearts, as in the provocation, in the day of temptation in the wilderness . . .

b. Makes Christ Known

1 Corinthians 12:3
Wherefore I give you to understand, that no man speaking by the Spirit of God calleth Jesus accursed; and that no man can say that Jesus is the Lord, but by the Holy Ghost.

John 16:14,15
He shall glorify me; for he shall receive of mine, and shall show it unto you. All things that the Father hath are mine; therefore said I, that he shall take of mine, and shall show it unto you.

a. Convicts of Sin

John 16:8
"When he comes, he will convict the world of guilt in regard to sin and righteousness and judgment."

Acts 7:51
"You stiff-necked people, with uncircumcised hearts and ears! You are just like your fathers: You always resist the Holy Spirit!"

Hebrews 3:7,8
So, as the Holy Spirit says: "Today, if you hear his voice, do not harden your hearts as you did in the rebellion, during the time of testing in the desert."

b. Makes Christ Known

1 Corinthians 12:3
Therefore I tell you that no one who is speaking by the Spirit of God says, "Jesus be cursed," and no one can say, "Jesus is Lord," except by the Holy Spirit.

John 16:14,15
"He will bring glory to me by taking from what is mine and making it known to you. All that belongs to the Father is mine. That is why I said the Spirit will take from what is mine and make it known to you."

c. Gives Assurance

Romans 8:16
The Spirit itself beareth witness with our spirit, that we are the children of God.

Galatians 4:6
And because ye are sons, God hath sent forth the Spirit of his Son into your hearts, crying, Abba, Father.

1 John 4:13
Hereby know we that we dwell in him, and he in us, because he hath given us of his Spirit.

1 John 5:9
If we receive the witness of men, the witness of God is greater; for this is the witness of God which he hath testified of his Son.

d. Gives Life

John 3:5
Jesus answered, Verily, verily, I say unto thee, Except a man be born of water and of the Spirit, he cannot enter into the kingdom of God.

John 6:63
It is the Spirit that quickeneth; the flesh profiteth nothing . . .

Romans 8:2
For the law of the Spirit of life in Christ Jesus hath made me free from the law of sin and death.

e. Seals Believers

Ephesians 1:13
In whom ye also trusted, after that ye heard the word of truth, the gospel of your salvation; in whom also, after that ye believed, ye were sealed with that Holy Spirit of promise . . .

Ephesians 4:30
And grieve not the holy Spirit of God, whereby ye are sealed unto the day of redemption.

c. Gives Assurance

Romans 8:16
The Spirit himself testifies with our spirit that we are God's children.

Galatians 4:6
Because you are sons, God sent the Spirit of his Son into our hearts, the Spirit who calls out, "Abba, Father."

1 John 4:13
We know that we live in him and he in us, because he has given us of his Spirit.

1 John 5:9
We accept man's testimony, but God's testimony is greater because it is the testimony of God, which he has given about his Son.

d. Gives Life

John 3:5
Jesus answered, "I tell you the truth, unless a man is born of water and the Spirit, he cannot enter the kingdom of God."

John 6:63
"The Spirit gives life; the flesh counts for nothing . . . "

Romans 8:2
Because through Christ Jesus the law of the Spirit of life set me free from the law of sin and death.

e. Seals Believers

Ephesians 1:13
And you also were included in Christ when you heard the word of truth, the gospel of your salvation. Having believed, you were marked in him with a seal, the promised Holy Spirit . . .

Ephesians 4:30
And do not grieve the Holy Spirit of God, with whom you were sealed for the day of redemption.

f. Guarantees Our Salvation

2 Corinthians 5:5
Now he that hath wrought us for the selfsame thing is God, who also hath given unto us the earnest of the Spirit.

2 Corinthians 1:22
Who hath also sealed us, and given the earnest of the Spirit in our hearts.

Ephesians 1:14
Which is the earnest of our inheritance until the redemption of the purchased possession, unto the praise of his glory.

g. Teaches Through God's Word

John 14:26
But the Comforter, which is the Holy Ghost, whom the Father will send in my name, he shall teach you all things, and bring all things to your remembrance, whatsoever I have said unto you.

h. Leads Believers

Romans 8:14
For as many as are led by the Spirit of God, they are the sons of God.

Galatians 5:18
But if ye be led of the Spirit, ye are not under the law.

i. Indwells Believers

1 Corinthians 3:16
Know ye not that ye are the temple of God, and that the Spirit of God dwelleth in you?

Romans 8:9
But ye are not in the flesh, but in the Spirit, if so be that the Spirit of God dwell in you. Now if any man have not the Spirit of Christ, he is none of his.

f. Guarantees Our Salvation

2 Corinthians 5:5
Now it is God who has made us for this very purpose and has given us the Spirit as a deposit, guaranteeing what is to come.

2 Corinthians 1:22
Set his seal of ownership on us, and put his Spirit in our hearts as a deposit, guaranteeing what is to come.

Ephesians 1:14
Who is a deposit guaranteeing our inheritance until the redemption of those who are God's possession—to the praise of his glory.

g. Teaches Through God's Word

John 14:26
"But the Counselor, the Holy Spirit, whom the Father will send in my name, will teach you all things and will remind you of everything I have said to you."

h. Leads Believers

Romans 8:14
Because those who are led by the Spirit of God are sons of God.

Galatians 5:18
But if you are led by the Spirit, you are not under law.

i. Indwells Believers

1 Corinthians 3:16
Don't you know that you yourselves are God's temple and that God's Spirit lives in you?

Romans 8:9
You, however, are controlled not by the sinful nature but by the Spirit, if the Spirit of God lives in you. And if anyone does not have the Spirit of Christ, he does not belong to Christ.

j. Enables Us in Service

Acts 1:8
But ye shall receive power, after that the Holy Ghost is come upon
you . . .

Luke 24:49
And, behold, I send the promise of my Father upon you; but tarry
ye in the city of Jerusalem, until ye be endued with power from
on high.

Zechariah 4:6
Then he answered and spake unto me, saying, . . . Not by might,
nor by power, but by my Spirit, saith the Lord of hosts.

John 15:5
 . . . for without me ye can do nothing.

j. Enables Us in Service

Acts 1:8
"But you will receive power when the Holy Spirit comes on you . . ."

Luke 24:49
"I am going to send you what my Father has promised; but stay in the city until you have been clothed with power from on high."

Zechariah 4:6
So he said to me, . . . "Not by might nor by power, but by my Spirit," says the Lord Almighty.

John 15:5
" . . . apart from me you can do nothing."

Evidences of Our Salvation

a. We Walk in the Light

1 John 1:7
But if we walk in the light, as he is in the light, we have fellowship one with another, and the blood of Jesus Christ his Son cleanseth us from all sin.

b. We Keep His Commandments

1 John 2:3
And hereby we do know that we know him, if we keep his commandments.

John 15:14
Ye are my friends, if ye do whatsoever I command you.

c. We Love the Brethren

1 John 3:14
We know that we have passed from death unto life, because we love the brethren . . .

1 John 4:7
Beloved, let us love one another; for love is of God; and every one that loveth is born of God, and knoweth God.

d. We Love Not the World

1 John 2:15
Love not the world, neither the things that are in the world. If any

a. We Walk in the Light

1 John 1:7
But if we walk in the light, as he is in the light, we have fellowship with one another, and the blood of Jesus, his Son, purifies us from every sin.

b. We Keep His Commandments

1 John 2:3
We know that we have come to know him if we obey his commands.

John 15:14
"You are my friends if you do what I command."

c. We Love the Brethren

1 John 3:14
We know that we have passed from death to life, because we love our brothers . . .

1 John 4:7
Dear friends, let us love one another, for love comes from God. Everyone who loves has been born of God and knows God.

d. We Love Not the World

1 John 2:15
Do not love the world or anything in the world. If anyone loves the

man love the world, the love of the Father is not in him.

e. We Do Not Practice Sin

1 John 3:9
Whosoever is born of God doth not commit sin; for his seed re-
maineth in him; and he cannot sin, because he is born of God.

f. We Believe in Jesus

1 John 5:1,13
Whosoever believeth that Jesus is the Christ is born of God; and
every one that loveth him that begat loveth him also that is begotten
of him . . . These things have I written unto you that believe on
the name of the Son of God; that ye may know that ye have eternal
life, and that ye may believe on the name of the Son of God.

g. We Overcome the World

1 John 5:4,5
For whatsoever is born of God overcometh the world; and this is
the victory that overcometh the world, even our faith. Who is he
that overcometh the world, but he that believeth that Jesus is the
Son of God?

h. We Live Righteously

Titus 3:8
This is a faithful saying, and these things I will that thou affirm
constantly, that they which have believed in God might be careful
to maintain good works. These things are good and profitable unto
men.

world, the love of the Father is not in him.

e. We Do Not Practice Sin

1 John 3:9
No one who is born of God will continue to sin, because God's
seed remains in him; he cannot go on sinning, because he has been
born of God.

f. We Believe in Jesus

1 John 5:1,13
Everyone who believes that Jesus is the Christ is born of God, and
everyone who loves the father loves his child as well . . . I write
these things to you who believe in the name of the Son of God so
that you may know that you have eternal life.

g. We Overcome the World

1 John 5:4,5
For everyone born of God has overcome the world. This is the victory that has overcome the world, even our faith. Who is it that over-
comes the world? Only he who believes that Jesus is the Son of God.

h. We Live Righteously

Titus 3:8
This is a trustworthy saying. And I want you to stress these things,
so that those who have trusted in God may be careful to devote
themselves to doing what is good. These things are excellent and
profitable for everyone.